# Tongue Untwisters

## Darrell Pearson

## Mark Oestreicher

David C. Cook Church Ministries—Resources
A division of Cook Communications Ministries
Colorado Springs, CO/Paris, Ontario

Custom Curriculum
Tongue Untwisters

© 1994, 1998 David C. Cook Publishing Co.

David C. Cook Church Ministries—Resources
A division of Cook Communications Ministries
4050 Lee Vance View; Colorado Springs, CO 80918-7100
www.cookministries.com
Series creator: John Duckworth
Series editor: Randy Southern
Editor: Randy Southern
Option writers: Stan Campbell, John Duckworth, Sue Reck, and Randy Southern
Designer: Bill Paetzold
Cover illustrator: Joe Weissmann
Inside illustrator: Joe Weissmann
Printed in U.S.A.

ISBN: 0-7814-5149-3

# CONTENTS

Sessions by Mark Oestreicher
Options by Stan Campbell, John Duckworth, Sue Reck, and Randy Southern

# About the Authors

**Mark Oestreicher** is a junior high pastor in Pasadena, California, as well as a seminar leader and author.

**Stan Campbell** has been a youth worker for almost twenty years and has written several books on youth ministry including the BibleLog series (SonPower) and the Quick Studies series (David C. Cook). Among the books he's written in the Custom Curriculum series are *Hormone Helper, Just Look at You! What Would Jesus Do?* and *Your Bible's Alive!* Stan and his wife, Pam, are youth directors at Lisle Bible Church in Lisle, Illinois.

**John Duckworth** is a writer and illustrator in Carol Stream, Illinois. He has worked with teenagers in youth groups and Sunday school, written several books including *The School Zone* (SonPower) and *Face to Face with Jesus* (in the Custom Curriculum series), and created such youth resources as Hot Topics Youth Electives and Snap Sessions for David C. Cook.

**Sue Reck** is an editor for Chariot Family Products. She is also a freelance curriculum writer. She has worked with young people in Sunday school classes, youth groups, and camp settings.

**Randy Southern** is a product developer of youth material at David C. Cook and the series editor of Custom Curriculum. He has also worked on such products as Quick Studies, Incredible Meeting Makers, Snap Sessions, First Aid for Youth Groups, Junior Highs Only, and Pathfinder Electives.

# You've Made the Right Choice!

Thanks for choosing **Custom Curriculum!** We think your choice says at least three things about you:

(1) You know your group pretty well, and want your program to fit that group like a glove;

(2) You like having options instead of being boxed in by some far-off curriculum editor;

(3) You have a small mole on your left forearm, exactly two inches below the elbow.

OK, so we were wrong about the mole. But if you like having choices that help you tailor meetings to fit your kids, **Custom Curriculum** *is* the best place to be.

## Going through Customs

In this (and every) **Custom Curriculum** volume, you'll find

• five great sessions you can use anytime, in any order.

• reproducible student handouts, at least one per session.

• a truckload of options for adapting the sessions to your group (more about that in a minute).

• a helpful get-you-ready article by a youth expert.

• clip art for making posters, fliers, and other kinds of publicity to get kids to your meetings.

Each **Custom Curriculum** session has three to six steps. No matter how many steps a session has, it's designed to achieve these goals:

• *Getting together.* Using an icebreaker activity, you'll help kids to be glad they came to the meeting.

• *Getting thirsty.* Why should kids care about your topic? Why should they care what the Bible has to say about it? You'll want to take a few minutes to earn their interest before you start pouring the "living water."

• *Getting the Word.* By exploring and discussing carefully selected passages, you'll find out what God has to say.

• *Getting the point.* Here's where you'll help kids make the leap from principles to nitty-gritty situations they are likely to face.

• *Getting personal.* What should each group member do as a result of this session? You'll help each person find a specific "next step" response that works for him or her.

Each session is written to last 45 to 60 minutes. But what if you have less time—or more? No problem! **Custom Curriculum** is all about . . . options!

# What Are My Options?

Every **Custom Curriculum** session gives you fourteen kinds of options:

• *Extra Action*—for groups that learn better when they're physically moving (instead of just reading, writing, and discussing).

• *Combined Junior High/High School*—to use when you're mixing age levels, and an activity or case study would be too "young" or "old" for part of the group.

• *Small Group*—for adapting activities that would be tough with groups of fewer than eight kids.

• *Large Group*—to alter steps for groups of more than twenty kids.

• *Urban*—for fitting sessions to urban facilities and multiethnic (especially African-American) concerns.

• *Heard It All Before*—for fresh approaches that get past the defenses of kids who are jaded by years in church.

• *Little Bible Background*—to use when most of your kids are strangers to the Bible, or haven't made a Christian commitment.

• *Mostly Guys*—to focus on guys' interests and to substitute activities they might be more enthused about.

• *Mostly Girls*—to address girls' concerns and to substitute activities they might prefer.

• *Extra Fun*—for longer, more "rowdy" youth meetings where the emphasis is on fun.

• *Short Meeting Time*—tips for condensing the session to 30 minutes or so.

• *Fellowship & Worship*—for building deeper relationships or enabling kids to praise God together.

• *Media*—to spice up meetings with video, music, or other popular media.

• *Sixth Grade*—appearing only in junior high/middle school volumes, this option helps you change steps that sixth graders might find hard to understand or relate to.

• *Extra Challenge*—appearing only in high school volumes, this option lets you crank up the voltage for kids who are ready for more Scripture or more demanding personal application.

Each kind of option is offered at least twice in each session. So in this book, you get *almost 150* ways to tweak the meetings to fit your group!

# Customizing a Session

*All right,* you may be thinking. *With all of these options flying around, how do I put a session together? I don't have a lot of time, you know.*

We know! That's why we've made **Custom Curriculum** as easy to follow as possible. Let's take a look at how you might prepare an actual meeting. You can do that in four easy steps:

(1) *Read the basic session plan.* Start by choosing one or more of the goals listed at the beginning of the session. You have three to pick from: a goal that emphasizes *knowledge,* one that stresses *understanding,* and one that emphasizes *action.* Choose one or more, depending on what *you* want to accomplish. Then read the basic plan to see what will work for you and what might not.

(2) *Choose your options.* You don't *have* to use any options at all; the

basic session plan would work well for many groups, and you may want to stick with it if you have absolutely no time to consider options. But if you want a more perfect fit, check out your choices.

As you read the basic session plan, you'll see small symbols in the margin. Each symbol stands for a different kind of option. When you see a symbol, it means that kind of option is offered for that step. Turn to the options section (which can be found immediately following the Repro Resources for each session), look for the category indicated by the symbol, and you'll see that option explained.

Let's say you have a small group, mostly guys who get bored if they don't keep moving. You'll want to keep an eye out for three kinds of options: Small Group, Mostly Guys, and Extra Action. As you read the basic session, you might spot symbols that tell you there are Small Group options for Step 1 and Step 3—maybe a different way to play a game so that you don't need big teams, and a way to cover several Bible passages when just a few kids are looking them up. Then you see symbols telling you that there are Mostly Guys options for Step 2 and Step 4—perhaps a substitute activity that doesn't require too much self-disclosure, and a case study guys will relate to. Finally you see symbols indicating Extra Action options for Step 2 and Step 3—maybe an active way to get kids' opinions instead of handing out a survey, and a way to act out some verses instead of just looking them up.

After reading the options, you might decide to use four of them. You base your choices on your personal tastes and the traits of your group that you think are most important right now. **Custom Curriculum** offers you more options than you'll need, so you can pick your current favorites and plug others into future meetings if you like.

(3) *Use the checklist.* Once you've picked your options, keep track of them with the simple checklist that appears at the end of each option section (just before the start of the next session plan). This little form gives you a place to write down the materials you'll need, too—since they depend on the options you've chosen.

(4) *Get your stuff together.* Gather your materials; photocopy any Repro Resources (reproducible student sheets) you've decided to use. And . . . you're ready!

# The Custom Curriculum Challenge

Your kids are fortunate to have you as their leader. You see them not as a bunch of generic teenagers, but as real, live, unique kids. You care whether you really connect with them. That's why you're willing to take a few extra minutes to tailor your meetings to fit.

It's a challenge to work with real, live kids, isn't it? We think you deserve a standing ovation for taking that challenge. And we pray that **Custom Curriculum** helps you shape sessions that shape lives for Jesus Christ and His kingdom.

**—The Editors**

# The Power of Words

## by Darrell Pearson

There are roughly 615,000 words that the Oxford English Dictionary lists as belonging to the English language. That's a lot of words. And that number doesn't include the nuances of meaning within words that give them such variety and texture. Nor does it include specialty words, such as those science puzzlers that only three people in the world use.

So why is everybody always saying the wrong thing? Aren't there enough words to choose from to find just the right thing to say?

### Mouths in Action

Obviously, everyone suffers from the malady of inappropriate speech, but teenagers just might have the disease in the worst possible way. Perhaps the reason is that they have knowledge of only, say, 598,000 words—and the really *nice* ones are yet to be learned. Or maybe kids simply lack the wisdom and ability to carefully select the proper word for the correct situation. Regardless, young people are always having trouble with the things they say.

Here's where you come in. Being an adult leader with a complete working knowledge of 615,000 words, not to mention the adept social graces to use them accurately, you are in the unique situation of being able to help your group members come to grips with their lips, so to speak. Or, if you don't feel like you actually know a half million plus words, there's certainly some good news in this book, because it's chock full of practical advice for group members to learn how to better shape what comes out of their mouths.

I'll never forget when an eighth grader named Matt was chosen to come up front for a summer camp game. When a girl of the same age was chosen to assist, Matt exclaimed, "Not her! She's ugly!" I've often wondered what effect those cruel words had on this young lady who had to endure the embarrassment of 175 people staring at her to judge whether his words were true. (By the way, Matt was no physical dream-come-true.) Matt's words hurt her, and had he understood that simple fact—or cared—one young lady's view of the world that week would have been different. I'm sure that Matt never intended to hurt her. He was just speaking the truth as he saw it, though certainly not in love.

This is what teenagers do. They are constantly getting themselves into trouble with their mouths—whether it's with parents, friends, teachers, or youth leaders. *They* don't always like what they say, either; but they are so quick to talk before thinking that they put themselves in regrettable circumstances.

### Tongue Tips

Here are a few thoughts that might help you help your group members as you work through the material in this book.

• *Stopping a group member in mid-sentence is sometimes OK. Our* tendency is to let kids talk when they've been asked a question (after all, we want to build their self-image), and generally, it's a good thing to let them do just that, even when the answer is hard to interpret or is on the wrong subject. But when it comes to kids publicly saying something that can be hurtful to others, don't hesitate to stop them or ignore them. Often they just want to see the shock value of their words, and you don't have to pander to their motivations.

We have this problem once in a while at our *Next Exit* junior high events. We often send a microphone into the audience to get kids' thoughts on the subject at hand, and occasionally we find ourselves in the uncomfortable situation of having to deal with an inappropriate or offensive remark. We've found it best not to respond, not to make a joke out of it, but to simply ignore it or stop it and move on. (We also hang on to the microphone to retain control while the young person talks.) The audience is able to easily and comfortably adjust and move on to the next person's response. If you need to, don't hesitate to stop a young person in mid-sentence if it will prevent someone else from being offended.

• *Some offensive language is a given with some group members.* Junior high ministry in particular has never been for the squeamish or faint of heart. The leader who blows up at every offensive statement does not understand this age group. Much of the time, the words that come out of kids' mouths come out with different intentions, but somehow the phrase gets all messed up in the delivery. Determine if the words you are hearing are intended to be hurtful, or if the person has just said something that he or she doesn't mean. Don't be too hard on the kid who is really trying.

I once finished a brilliant (in my perspective) Sunday school lesson with an eighth-grade class. The students were spellbound (well, they were bound). When I finished, I asked if there were any questions. There was a short pause, and then a very pleasant girl raised her hand. "What time is this over?" She didn't mean to be hurtful, she just wanted to know when I was done. It never crossed her mind that I might be a little hurt after my significant effort. Try to remind yourself that part of the joy of working with junior and senior highers is their straightforward honesty.

• *Focus on the positive things you hear.* We don't reward kids often enough for the times they *do* say the right thing, and instead simply harp on them when they blow it. I read a phrase a few years ago in the book *The One Minute Manager* that has always helped me in this area: "Help people reach their full potential; catch them doing something right." When a junior higher strokes someone else with their words or comments positively about another's dress or behavior, notice it and tell them you were impressed. Your reinforcement of their choice of words will be remembered.

• *Model good word choice yourself.* How many times have you said something to your group members that you later regretted? ("OK, kids, today we're—*hey, shut up!!*—talking about—*I said, shut up!!!*—about choosing your words carefully . . .") Think about what you're going to say ahead of time, and show kids with your carefully chosen words how it's supposed to be done.

It takes great patience sometimes to choose your words carefully. But you can bet that your kids will be listening closely to what you say and how you tame your own tongue. I still remember an incident when I was in high school in which a youth director responded very inappropriately to a young person. It was the beginning of the end for the leader; his credibility and our respect for him diminished remarkably after his ill-chosen words.

• *Create symbols or signs for your group that signify that it's time to be quiet or time to give someone a verbal stroke.* The sign could be a hand in front of the face, or a thumb up, or an index finger to the ear. Create one that you will use consistently and that will become a code signal for the whole group. Be willing to follow it yourself when someone shows *you* the sign.

• *Be aware that the verbal modeling kids get at home is often very poor.* With so many young people living in unusual family situations, frequently they reflect what they hear all of the time at home. A ninth-grade guy once told me that the best sexual advice he ever got from his stepdad was "Use it or lose it." No wonder he struggled with choosing appropriate words.

• *Teach the words of Jesus.* Make sure that you often have group members learn and read the words of Jesus. Remind them that Jesus' words were never boring, but full of wit, truth, honesty, concern, and challenge. They were also never inappropriate.

I've noticed that my closest adult friends—ones that have been long-time Christians—will often use a short phrase from Scripture in a humorous or meaningful way. They don't think about it; it just flows out of them. It comes from years of absorbing the Word. Help your kids to do just that. Teach them not to just *live* like Jesus, but to *sound* like Him as well. I don't know if Jesus knew 615,000 words in Aramaic, but I know that of the ones He did know, He chose them carefully.

*Darrell Pearson is co-founder of 10 TO 20, an organization headquartered in Colorado Springs that creates high-involvement youth events for teenagers, including* Next Exit, *a junior high program that tours the U.S. and Canada each year.*

The images on these two pages are designed to help you promote this course within your church and community. Feel free to photocopy anything here and adapt it to fit your publicity needs. The stuff on this page could be used as a flier that you send or hand out to kids—or as a bulletin insert. The stuff on the next page could be used to add visual interest to newsletters, calendars, bulletin boards, or other promotions. Be creative and have fun!

# Has Your Mouth Ever Gotten You in Trouble?

Swearing, telling dirty jokes, cutting others down, gossiping, lying—these are just a few of the many ways that the tongue can cause problems. How can we control such a powerful weapon? Find out as we begin a new series called *Tongue Untwisters.*

**Who:**

**When:**

**Where:**

**Questions? Call:**

# Tongue Untwisters

## Tongue Untwisters

If you can't say something nice . . .

The dark side of humor

"Did you hear about . . . ?"

# The Dark Side of Humor

## YOUR GOALS FOR THIS SESSION:

*Choose one or more*

☐ To help kids recognize how inappropriate humor can be destructive.

☐ To help kids understand the difference between constructive humor and destructive humor.

☐ To help kids make a commitment to use constructive humor instead of destructive humor.

☐ Other _____

## Your Bible Base:

Ephesians 5:4
James 3:7-10

STEP

I

# Funny Bone

*(Needed: Adult volunteer, chalkboard and chalk or newsprint and marker, prizes)*

Have kids form two or three teams. If possible, try to use some natural divisions when forming the teams. For instance, you might have guys against girls. Or you might have a sixth-grade team, a seventh-grade team, and an eighth-grade team.

Instruct the members of each team to pull their chairs together. Have the teams separate themselves from each other as much as possible. Give the teams five minutes to come up with three jokes. Emphasize that the jokes *must* be clean. Announce that each joke must be told by a different representative from the team.

You'll need to find an adult volunteer to serve as an impartial judge for this activity. This person will award points for each joke on a scale of −100 to +100. Racist humor, sexual innuendoes, or any other inappropriate joke should receive negative points. Encourage your judge to be generous with the positive points. Most group members probably won't be able to tell a joke like a comedian, so any reasonably funny joke should receive over 75 points. Even dumb jokes should receive some points.

After five minutes, bring the teams together. Explain the point system and display the prizes that the teams will be competing for. Then have a representative from the first team stand up and tell his or her joke. The judge's score should be announced immediately and displayed on the board.

Be sure to encourage all of the joke-tellers—after all, many kids probably won't want to fill this role. Having group members tell the jokes will be fun for your kids, no matter how dumb the jokes are. It will also save you from attempting to tell a few jokes that will confirm the kids' suspicions about you!

After all of the representatives have told their jokes, total the points and award the prizes to the winning team.

# The Anatomy of Funny

*(Needed: VCR and videotape [optional])*

Tell some kind of humorous story about your life—preferably a time when you did something really stupid or a time when something really funny happened to you. Allow group members to laugh at you. (Chances are that kids may not need much prompting to do this.)

Then ask for volunteers to share stories of times when something really funny happened to them. (Depending on the size and comfort-level of your group, you may or may not get responses to this.) Be sure to provide support and encouragement to any kids who are brave enough to share.

Afterward, ask: **What's the funniest movie you've ever seen? What made it funny?** Get several responses.

**What movie tried to be funny, but was really dumb? Why wasn't it funny?** Get several responses.

**What's the funniest TV show on right now? Why is it funny?** Get several responses.

If you have time, it would be great to show a Ren and Stimpy cartoon or some other short, off-the-wall video. Afterward, ask the kids what parts were funny and why.

# Distorted Funny

*(Needed: Bibles, chalkboard and chalk or newsprint and marker, an out-of-focus picture or a pair of binoculars)*

Hold up an out-of-focus picture. Ask: **What's wrong with this picture?** (It's out of focus; it's blurry.)

**Is an out-of-focus picture as good as one that is clearly focused? Why not?** (You can't see an out-of-focus picture as well as you can see an in-focus picture. Out-of-focus pictures bother the eyes.)

If you can't find an out-of-focus picture, use binoculars instead. Make the binoculars as out-of-focus as possible. Then have two or three group members look through the lens and comment on what's wrong.

Afterward, say: **There are many things in our world that God made really good, but that Satan has distorted or made "out-of-focus" and turned into something bad. Can you think of some examples?** (God created music, but sometimes it gets distorted and becomes bad. God made sex, but it often gets distorted and becomes badly used. Another obvious connection is humor.)

**How do you think God feels about humor?** (Perhaps He enjoys some forms of humor, but He certainly frowns upon other types of humor.)

**Can humor be a good thing? Explain.** (Yes. Laughter can brighten a person's mood.)

**Is there anything good that God didn't create?** (No. All good things come from God.)

Draw a circle in the middle of your board. Write the word "good" in it. Then explain: **God wants our lives to be filled with joy. He made us to enjoy humor. Little babies can laugh long before they can talk. It's likely that there will be a lot of laughter in heaven.**

Write the word "humor" in the circle on the board. Then say: **But because Satan can't create anything on his own, he tries to distort God's good stuff—he makes things "out-of-focus."**

**What are some ways that humor can get distorted and become destructive?** (When it makes fun of people; when it uses sexual language that's wrong; when it tears down another race or perpetuates any kind of stereotypes.) List group members' answers on the board to the right of the circle.

Have kids form three groups. Assign each group one of the following Scripture passages: James 3:9, 10; Ephesians 5:4; and James 3:7, 8. Instruct each group to read its passage and discuss what the passage has to do with distorted or destructive humor.

After a few minutes, have each group share its conclusions. Use the following information to supplement your discussion of the passages.

• *James 3:9, 10*—We're all made in God's likeness. When we joke about other people, not only are we hurting them, we're insulting God's craftsmanship.

• *Ephesians 5:4*—This is a clear command not to be involved in sexual humor.

• *James 3:7, 8*—We can do a lot of destruction and damage to people with inappropriate joking.

Afterward, say: **Satan can really distort God's good creation of humor with this destructive stuff.** Point to the words and phrases you wrote to the right of the circle on the board. **Satan's very tricky. Just when we figure out how he's distorting God's**

**truth in one direction, he'll distort it in a completely differ-
ent direction.** Point to the blank space to the left of the circle.

Ask: **If we're careful to avoid destructive humor, what's
another way Satan could distort God's good creation of
humor?** This question may be a little hard for your kids. If they can't
come up with any ideas, ask: **Have you ever met a Christian
who's being so careful to avoid bad humor that he or she
refuses to have any fun at all?**

After you get a few responses, write "No Humor" to the left of the
circle on the board. Then summarize: **God made humor. He made
us to laugh. But Satan would love to distort that—to make it
out-of-focus—in either direction. Satan would love you to
live a boring life with no humor or joy at all. He'd also love
you to involve yourself in a lot of destructive humor—listening and telling jokes and funny stories that are sexual, racial,
mean, or even that mock God Himself.**

# What's Good, What's Not?

*(Needed: Copies of Repro Resource 1, pencils)*

Hand out copies of "Humor Meter" (Repro Resource 1) and pencils.
Say: **Let's see how good your judgment is. Some humor is
obviously good and some humor is obviously destructive. But
some humor isn't obvious at all. Draw a needle on each of
the humor meters on this sheet to indicate how good or
destructive you think that humor is.**

Give kids a few minutes to complete the sheet. When everyone is
finished, go through the sheet one situation at a time, asking kids to
share their responses for each humor meter. If you get varying results,
ask kids to explain their responses. Encourage kids with strong feelings
about a particular situation to debate the issue, but don't let arguments
get out of hand.

# Moving Forward

*(Needed: Copies of Repro Resource 2, pencils)*

OPTIONS

Say: **Our world is full of destructive humor—and Satan makes sure that a lot of that destructive humor seems really fun to us.**

Hand out copies of "The Humor Highway" (Repro Resource 2). It would be great if you could copy this back-to-back with Repro Resource 1. Say: **Because this is such a tough area, let's think about taking one step forward on the "humor highway" this week.**

Have group members take a few minutes to privately mark where they would honestly place themselves on the Humor Highway diagram right now. Assure them that you won't be collecting these papers and that no one will see their answers.

Then say: **If you are willing to commit yourself to God to try to move one step forward on the diagram this week, draw a little arrow from where you first marked to where you'll try to be by the end of next week.** Instruct kids to sign their names next to the arrow to symbolize their commitment.

Close the session in prayer, asking God to give your group members strength to keep these commitments and to give them many opportunities to enjoy good humor the way He made it.

# HUMOR METER

*Draw a needle on each humor meter to indicate how good or destructive you think that type of humor is.*

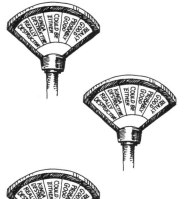

1. Your best friend tells you a dumb "knock-knock" joke.

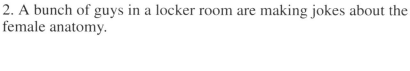

2. A bunch of guys in a locker room are making jokes about the female anatomy.

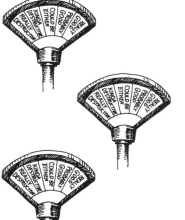

3. A kid at your lunch table starts a joke by saying, "There was a Jew and a black guy walking down the street . . ."

4. You tell your brother that your parents want to sell him to a family overseas.

5. You and your friends are laughing about the size of your art teacher's nose.

6. A Christian kid from your youth group tells you a joke about Jesus stealing from someone.

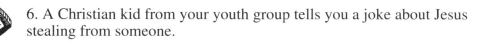

7. A comedian on TV tells a whole series of jokes about having sex with her boyfriend.

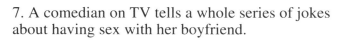

8. You're reading the Sunday comics, and one of them about a caveman really cracks you up.

Step 1: Place a mark on the highway to reflect your actions last week.
Step 2: Draw a little arrow toward where you'd like to be by the end of next week.
Step 3: Sign your name by the arrow as a symbol of your commitment to God.

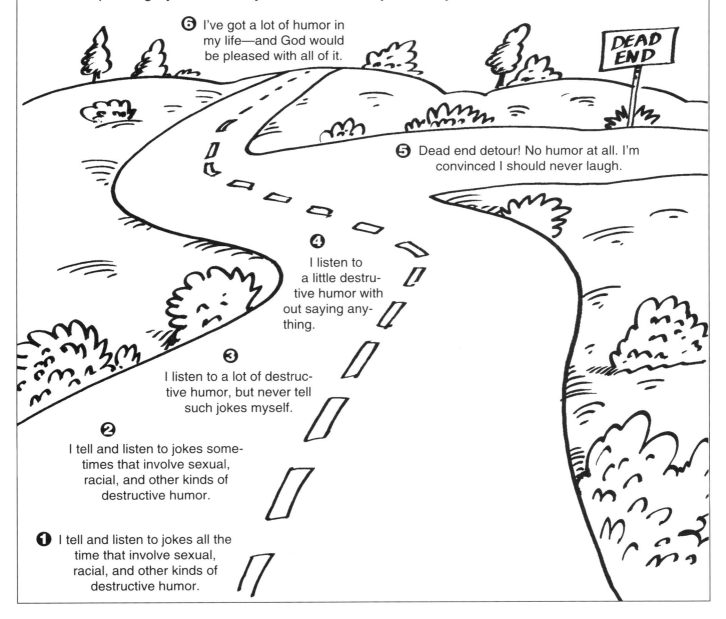

## Step 1

Try one or more of the following activities. (1) *Side-splitting Contest.* Give each team a trash bag and plenty of pillows. Have each team stuff pillows into its bag until the bag splits. The first team to "split a side" wins. (2) *Knee-slapping Contest.* Have kids sit in a circle. Slap your knees twice in a pattern (two quick slaps; one soft slap and one loud one; etc.). The next person must duplicate your pattern and add another. Work your way around the circle, with each person matching and adding. Anyone who makes a mistake is out; the last player left wins. (3) *Rib-tickling Contest.* Have your guys stand up. At your signal, girls will tickle them in the ribs. Any guy who can last for one minute without laughing gets a prize. Afterward, ask: **What kind of humor is side-splitting, knee-slapping, or rib-tickling to you? What kind of humor leaves you cold? Why?**

## Step 3

Give each person a newspaper cartoon. Let kids go outside and "turn a clean joke into a dirty one" by rubbing their cartoons in the dirt. Then challenge kids to "clean up" their jokes with soap and water—a difficult task. In Step 4, cut situations 2-6 from Repro Resource 1; put each situation in an envelope. Address each envelope to someone who could be hurt by each joke ("Female," "Jewish or African-American person," "Brother," etc.). Hide the envelopes. Explain that whoever finds an envelope must take on the identity written on the envelope, read the situation, and consider how the joke could hurt him or her. In Step 5, have teams run a "Lighten Up" relay race. Each runner should wear a backpack filled with weights. Label each weight with a type of inappropriate humor ("sexual jokes," "racial slurs," etc.). Each runner may take out any weights whose corresponding types of humor he or she promises to avoid this week.

## Step 1

Rather than having kids form teams for the opening activity, try a different approach. Hand out paper and pencils. Instruct each person to write down his or her favorite inoffensive joke. After a few minutes, collect the papers. Read each joke aloud, trying to make it sound as funny as possible. As your impartial judge is rating the joke according to the scale described in the session plan, group members should try to guess whose joke it is. After the joke writer has been identified, have the judge reveal his or her score for the joke.

## Step 2

To expand the scope of the humorous anecdote activity for a small group, let each person tell *two* stories about himself or herself—one that's true and one that's made-up. After each person tells his or her stories, the rest of the group members should vote for the one they think is the true story. If they wish, they can keep score to see who is best at separating truth from lies. They might also want to determine who is the best (funniest) storyteller in the group.

## Step 2

With a large group, you're likely to have some "performers" in your midst. Give them a chance to put their talents to use by acting out some scenes from the funniest movies or TV shows they've ever seen. Emphasize that the scenes must be suitable (non-offensive, not suggestive) to perform in front of the group. Let kids work in pairs or small groups to prepare their presentations; then give each group one minute to perform.

## Step 3

Rather than holding up an out-of-focus picture, make the same point in another way. You'll need a music tape and a tape player with volume, bass, and treble controls. Announce that you've heard a great new song that you want your group members to hear. However, when you play the tape, turn up (or down) the bass and treble levels so that the song is completely distorted. Use this example to introduce the idea of distorted humor.

**HEARD IT ALL BEFORE**

**LITTLE BIBLE BACKGROUND**

**FELLOWSHIP & WORSHIP**

### Step 3

The Bible's opposition to certain kinds of humor probably is no surprise to kids. But they may wonder *why* these things are off limits, especially when "inappropriate" humor is used by most peers and adults. You may want to make the following points. (1) **Why is sexual humor off limits? Because sex is "dirty"? No. Sex was created by God, so it's good. But it's reserved for people who are married to each other. Most sexual jokes imply that sex outside of marriage is funny. Or they describe activities that unmarried people shouldn't be discussing with each other—either because the discussion revs up their sexual fantasies, or because it implies that it's cool to be sexually experienced whether you're married or not.**
(2) **Why is "mean" humor off limits? Shouldn't people realize we're only joking? It's true that we see a lot of "funny" put-downs on TV sitcoms. If we were all fictional characters, maybe "insult" humor would be OK. But we're not. We have feelings, and feelings get hurt. Christians are supposed to put others' needs ahead of their own, even if it means having to skip a really "clever" remark about someone who's "hypersensitive."**

### Step 5

Jaded kids may mark (or ignore) Repro Resource 2 and forget the whole thing before you close in prayer. Make the exercise a little harder to forget by bringing a "smiley face" rubber stamp (or any stamp featuring a laughing or smiling character) and an ink pad. Have kids stamp their Repro Resources instead of drawing arrows, and then stamp the backs of their own hands as a reminder of what they did.

### Step 3

Explain to your kids that back in the "old" days, McDonald's promoted the Big Mac sandwich as "Two all-beef patties, special sauce, lettuce, cheese, pickles, onions, on a sesame seed bun." The promotion worked because the ads were run frequently, contests were held to see how quickly people could recite the phrase, and the slogan became a cool piece of information to know. See if any group members have memorized similarly complex, yet irrelevant information. Then explain that sometimes we (especially people with little Bible background) may assume that humor is never bad as long as no *actions* are taken. However, *words* can be wrong. Words that get embedded in our minds influence our thinking. Discuss the connection between attitudes and actions. Have kids repeat Philippians 4:8 a dozen times until it begins to stick in their minds: "Whatever is true, whatever is noble, whatever is right, whatever is pure, whatever is lovely, whatever is admirable—if anything is excellent or praiseworthy—think about such things." After kids memorize the verse, challenge them to think about what it means.

### Step 5

The Bible study in Step 3 may have been a bit jolting to kids who genuinely didn't know any better about improper joking around. To close, give kids the time and materials to make "flash cards" of the verses that most affected them and that they want to remember. Have them copy the verses on small cards to use as bookmarks, locker/mirror reminders, and so forth. Explain that change won't be easy, that they will need frequent reminders before they begin to see results.

### Step 1

Many kids—especially those who have grown up in the church—think all worship must be solemn and ceremoniously boring. They often don't see or hear that God wants us to *rejoice* in Him—to make a *joyful* noise unto Him. Before the session, prepare your meeting area for a worship celebration like your group members have never seen. Decorate with balloons and streamers, create a mood of celebration, and play some very upbeat worship and praise music. When the kids arrive, involve them in the music and celebration. After a few minutes, ask: **Did any of you ever think a worship service could be so joyful?** Get a few responses. Say: **God created joy and fun, just as He created everything else that's good. He wants us to have fun and enjoy life.** Then begin Step 1 in the session.

### Step 5

Set up a large paper "wall" on which kids can write "graffiti-style" their favorite jokes. Give kids markers, paint, or whatever else you have on hand. Then say: **We've just learned that God gave us the gift of humor and that there are good and not so good ways to use that gift. This wall is the "Champions Wall of Humor—proud sponsor of the U.S. Olympic Humor Team." On it, we are going to write our best fun stuff—jokes, humorous things that have happened to you, etc.** Let the kids go at it, making sure they use only appropriate humor. When they're done, hand out Good Humor ice cream bars, read the wall, and have a good laugh!

### Step 3

If your girls are open to sharing, ask: **How many of you can remember a time when you were on the receiving end of someone else's destructive humor?** Encourage those who share to describe how the experience made them feel. List the feelings that are described as group members share. Then ask: **For what purpose do you think God created humor?** As your girls share their thoughts, make another list. Afterward, compare the two lists and discuss the differences between them.

### Step 4

Change the situations on Repro Resource 1 as follows:
• 2. A bunch of girls are telling funny stories about a new girl who dresses and talks very differently than they do.
• 5. You and your friends are laughing at your youth leader's new haircut.
• 6. A Christian kid from your youth group tells a joke about the Virgin Mary.
After your group members have worked through Repro Resource 1, have them share some examples of situations they've been in that involved good or destructive humor. Discuss as a group how they reacted—or should have reacted.

### Step 4

After group members complete Repro Resource 1, focus your discussion on "locker room talk"—a problem that most guys will have to deal with. Ask: **Why do guys feel the need to get together and talk crudely about girls? Do** *you* **ever participate in locker room talk?** Point out that listening is participating. **Put yourself in the place of a girl who happened to overhear what was said about her. How would she feel? Would her feelings be justified? How would** *you* **feel about being evaluated purely on physical features?** Add other questions that you know would apply to your group of guys.

### Step 5

The application of the material covered in this session is a bit general. In many cases, guys tend to ignore opportunities unless they are spelled out clearly. So have your group members brainstorm specific ways to take one step forward on the "Humor Highway" this week. Ideas might include speaking up against the verbal abuse of others; countering negative comments with positive ones—at the risk of taking the brunt of the negative comments upon themselves; walking away from offensive people; and so on. Then ask each person to select one specific idea to put into practice this week. Close by motivating your guys with a personal challenge. Say: **What's the more manly thing to do: take part in cheap and hurtful humor or defend the dignity of someone else?**

### Step 1

Set up your room to suggest a comedy club's "Amateur Night," with a stage area and intimate seating for the spectators. Begin the meeting by letting kids take turns getting up and telling jokes. (Maintain the club atmosphere with applause, heckling, or whatever is appropriate.) You should make a list of the jokes that are told. Afterward, you can evaluate each one using the scoring system described in the session.

### Step 4

Introduce this step by showing some video clips (which you've pre-screened) from several recent movies. It shouldn't be hard to find examples of suggestive humor, put-downs of others, and so forth. After showing the clips, have kids work through Repro Resource 1. Wrap up this step by playing an audiocassette or a video of a Christian comedian performing clean humor that is truly funny. Let kids see that humor can be both enjoyable *and* uplifting if someone works at it hard enough.

### Step 1

Before the session, make an audio recording of a laughing audience (from a sound effects record or tape, a comedy album, or one of your pastor's funnier sermons). Make the recording at least a minute long, even if you have to record the same burst of laughter repeatedly. You'll be using this as a "laugh track" during your meeting. To start the session, play a one-minute, super-serious scene of a TV drama that you've recorded on your VCR; have your laugh track going at the same time and turn it up at inappropriate spots. Then ask: **How did this scene make you feel? Why? Are there some things in life that don't lend themselves to humor? If so, what? If not, why not?** You could also use your laugh track for the joke-telling contest by having your judge play the tape and turn the volume up and down to indicate scores.

### Step 3

To reinforce the idea that Christians don't have to be overly serious, play a contemporary Christian song that uses humor. Examples might include "I Want to Be a Clone" (Steve Taylor), "Fat Baby" (Amy Grant), "On One Condition" (Sonlight), and "Lookin' Out for Number One" (Wayne Watson). Or play a couple of minutes of comedy recorded by Christians such as Ken Davis, Bob Stromberg, Hicks and Cohagen, or Isaac Air Freight (check your Christian bookstore to see what's currently available).

### Step 1

Replace Steps 1 and 2 with a shorter opener called "Dueling Jokers." Before the session, cut humorous anecdotes and quotes from a copy of *Reader's Digest* or another family magazine. On a table at the front of your meeting place, put the clippings facedown in a pile. Have two group members come to the front. Each will choose a clipping and read it. The rest of the group will then vote on which item was funnier (cast tiebreaker votes yourself, if necessary). The reader of the losing item is declared "dead"; the winner picks another clipping and takes on another challenger. Keep track of who has the most wins in five minutes; give that person a prize, if you wish. Ask: **Why were some of these stories and quotes funnier than others? What kinds of humor do you like best?**

### Step 4

Instead of taking time to mark Repro Resource 1 and share results, try another option. Before the session, make a large version of a "humor meter" from the sheet, using cardboard and markers. Include the five headings and a moveable "needle" (fasten it with a brad or a piece of pipe cleaner). Have a volunteer come to the front of the room. Read the first situation from Repro Resource 1; then give kids ten seconds to call out their responses, trying to convince the volunteer where to move the needle. Let the volunteer decide what the majority opinion seems to be. In Step 5, hand out Repro Resource 2 for kids to take with them and mark later.

### Step 2

Spend some time talking about TV shows like HBO's "Def Comedy Jam" and others that feature sexual and racial humor targeted to an urban audience. Ask: **Why do you think so many people find that kind of humor funny and enjoyable? How do you feel about that type of humor? Why?**

### Step 4

Add the following examples to Repro Resource 1:
• A guy in your class starts telling a story using an exaggerated Hispanic accent.
• To get some laughs, you make a comment about the way a homeless person in your neighborhood is dressed.

## Step 1

Ask: **What really makes you laugh?** On a large sheet of paper, make two columns—one labeled "Junior High" and the other labeled "High School." As kids begin to share what tickles their funny bones, write their responses in the appropriate columns. When they've completed their lists, spend a moment discussing their answers, noting any differences between the two columns. Then say: **Our standards and what we find funny may change from time to time, but God's standards for humor, as for everything else, never change.**

## Step 4

Change the situations on Repro Resource 1 as follows:
• 2. A bunch of guys in the locker room are laughing about a new guy, making fun of his physical development.
• 5. At a restaurant, you and your friends laugh at a waiter who appears to be gay.
• 6. A Christian kid from your youth group tells you a joke about Jesus having sex with someone.

## Step 1

Your sixth graders may be a little shy about telling jokes on their own. To ease their minds a bit, give them joke books to use. Have the team representatives choose jokes from the joke books to read. If kids use jokes from the books, they may not be quite as embarrassed if they receive few points from the judge.

## Step 5

Rather than having your sixth graders fill out Repro Resource 2, try another option. Hand out Post-it™ Notes with some kind of "just a reminder" message on the front. Have kids write on their Post-it™ Note one thing they plan to do in the coming week to avoid destructive humor. Encourage kids to keep their Post-it™ Notes handy as a reminder of their commitment.

## Date Used:

Approx.
Time

**Step 1: Funny Bone** _____
o Extra Action
o Small Group
o Fellowship & Worship
o Extra Fun
o Media
o Short Meeting Time
o Combined Junior High/High School
o Sixth Grade
Things needed:

**Step 2: The Anatomy of Funny** _____
o Small Group
o Large Group
o Urban
Things needed:

**Step 3: Distorted Funny** _____
o Extra Action
o Large Group
o Heard It All Before
o Little Bible Background
o Mostly Girls
o Media
Things needed:

**Step 4: What's Good, What's Not?** _____
o Mostly Girls
o Mostly Guys
o Extra Fun
o Short Meeting Time
o Urban
o Combined Junior High/High School
Things needed:

**Step 5: Moving Forward** _____
o Heard It All Before
o Little Bible Background
o Fellowship & Worship
o Mostly Guys
o Sixth Grade
Things needed:

# SESSION 2

# Four-Letter Follies

## YOUR GOALS FOR THIS SESSION:

*Choose one or more*

- [ ] To help kids recognize why swearing is wrong.

- [ ] To help kids understand that the language they use is a reflection of their heart and mind.

- [ ] To help kids identify at least one area of "foul intake" to eliminate from their lives.

- [ ] Other _____

## Your Bible Base:

Exodus 20:7
Matthew 12:33, 34
Colossians 3:8, 17
James 1:26

O P T I O N S

EXTRA ACTION

SMALL GROUP

LARGE GROUP

FELLOWSHIP & WORSHIP

MOSTLY GIRLS

MOSTLY GUYS

EXTRA FUN

SHORT MEETING TIME

URBAN

SIXTH GRADE

## STEP 1

# Strange Transmission

*(Needed: Copies of Repro Resource 3, pencils)*

Hand out copies of "Strange Transmission" (Repro Resource 3) and pencils. Read aloud the instructions at the top of the sheet. Then have group members work in teams of three to complete the sheet. As kids work, walk around the room to make sure they understand what they're doing. The last thing you need is a group member taking home this sheet with actual swear words written all over it (unless you're hoping to get out of teaching junior high).

Give kids about five minutes to complete the sheet. When everyone is finished, have each team read the script it came up with.

Then ask: **What percent of the movies you see would you say have swearing in them? How do you feel about that kind of language in the movies you see?** Get several responses.

## STEP 2

# Don't Say It!

*(Needed: Two copies of Repro Resource 4, watch or clock with a second hand)*

Ask: **In what situations do junior highers you know swear?** (When they're surprised; when they hurt themselves; when they're mad at someone; when they want to sound tough.)

**Why do you think people choose to use a swear word instead of some other word?** (Because they like how the swear word sounds; because they want to shake people up; because it's the first word that comes to mind.)

Say: **It's possible that many people choose to use swear words because they're the first words that come to mind in certain situations. Most of us have probably heard people** who normally don't swear get surprised or hurt themselves and blurt out a swear word. Maybe some of you have done that by mistake. That's a pretty normal thing to do when you hear those words all the time. We're going to play a game now in which you can't say the first words that pop into your mind.

Have kids form two teams. Explain: **One at a time, I'll give you a card that has one word at the top written in capital letters. That's the word you will try to get your team to say. Below the word are five other words. These are five of the first words that would probably pop into your mind to describe the main word. You can't use any of these words or even any form of them. If you use one of these words, you lose the round. If your team guesses the main word in 10 seconds or less, you get three points. If you team guesses it in 10-20 seconds, you get two points. If your team guesses it in 20-30 seconds, you get one point. Thirty seconds is the maximum time. Also, you're not allowed to use any motions at all while you give clues.**

Call the first contestant from one team to the front of the room. Give him or her a card. Start the round within ten seconds. (You don't want the person to be able to think very long.) Be sure to have an extra copy of the card that you can look at to check for violations. If a player uses any form of the five words (or the key word), make a loud buzzing sound and tell the person that his or her team has lost the round. Make sure that you remind every contestant that he or she can't use any motions—this is really hard for kids.

Continue back and forth between the two teams until you've used all of the cards. Then total the points and announce the winning team.

**STEP 3**

# Squeaky Clean

*(Needed: Bibles)*

Ask: **What's wrong with swearing?** Get several responses.

**What makes a swear word a swear word?** Kids may offer answers like "because it's a dirty word" or "because it means something bad." These are somewhat true, but the real truth is that swear words are swear words in most cases because our culture decides they are.

**OPTIONS**

HEARD IT ALL BEFORE

LITTLE BIBLE BACKGROUND

MOSTLY GIRLS

MEDIA

SHORT MEETING TIME

**If we made up a swear word, when, if ever, would it move from being a pretend swear word to a real swear word?** (When our culture accepted it as a swear word.)

**If someone you're passing on the street says, "Jesus Christ," how would you know if he or she is swearing or talking about God's Son?**

**Why does God care if we swear or not?**

After several kids have responded, say: **Let's look at some verses in the Bible together.**

Have someone read aloud Colossians 3:8, 17. Then ask: **What does this passage say about swearing?** (It warns against "filthy language." Many swear words fall into this category.)

Have someone read aloud James 1:26. Then ask: **What does this verse say about swearing?** (It warns us to keep a "tight reign on [our] tongue." It also suggests that our Christianity is suspicious if we don't.)

Have someone read aloud Exodus 20:7. Many of your kids may know this verse because it's part of the Ten Commandments. Ask: **What does this verse say about swearing?** (It warns against using the Lord's name in vain. "In vain" means for no good reason.)

**How would you feel if your name became a common vulgar swear word? How do you think God feels about it?**

After you've gotten a few responses, say: **As you can see, God makes it pretty clear in the Bible that He doesn't like swearing. So every time we swear, it's kind of like saying to God, "I really don't care what You think."**

**OPTIONS**

EXTRA ACTION

LARGE GROUP

EXTRA FUN

URBAN

JR. HIGH / HIGH SCHOOL COMBINED

**STEP 4**

# A Difference of Opinions

*(Needed: Copies of Repro Resource 5, pencils)*

Hand out copies of "Opinions" (Repro Resource 5). Read each opinion aloud. Then have group members check one of the boxes— "Totally disagree," "Kinda disagree," "Kinda agree," or "Totally agree"— to indicate their response. After everyone has checked one of the boxes, have volunteers share their responses. Then, as a group, discuss the responses.

Say: **Think of five of your closest friends. Which of these opinions concerning swearing do you think is closest to the**

**opinions of your friends? Which opinion is closest to your opinion?** Volunteers may respond aloud if they wish, but you're really just asking group members to consider the questions silently.

# STEP 5

# Input-Output

*(Needed: Bibles)*

Remind group members of the game you played earlier in the session—the one in which contestants couldn't say most of the words that probably were the first to come to mind.

Say: **We've hinted at this a few times already, but we're going to take one last look at it. Simply knowing that swearing is wrong, and even deciding not to swear, may not be enough to really help some of you. Because you hear swearing so much, swear words are often the first words that come to your mind in certain situations. We take information in through our ears and keep it in two huge storage tanks—our mind and our heart.**

Have group members turn in their Bibles to Matthew 12:33, 34. Ask someone to read the passage aloud. This passage tells us that what comes out of our mouths is the overflow of our hearts. Suggest that we need to examine our input in order to help control our output.

Ask: **Where are some of the places you hear swearing?** (Friends, TV, movies, videos, music, family members, etc.)

**In which of these areas can you control how much input you receive? For instance, you might not be able to control the input level from a father who swears all the time, but you probably can control input from some of the other sources.**

To close the session, give your kids a minute or two to pray silently to God, asking Him to help them figure out how to cut down on the foul input in their lives.

# STRANGE TRANSMISSION

*Our church fax machine received a strange transmission the other day. As far as we can tell, it's a page from a movie script. But it seems to be an alien script. The fax machine must have known which words were swear words, because it left them all out. Your job is to come up with alien words to fill in the blanks. However, they can't be anything like any words you've heard here on earth.*

## The Torkshtuck Factor

*Characters:* Floit, the ultra-tough intergalactic cop; Crambot, the big-time intergalactic crime boss; Snorful, Floit's sidekick

**FLOIT:** Ah-hah, it's you, Crambot, you filthy _____. I knew we'd find your _____ hideout.

**SNORFUL:** Yeah, all I can say is _____.

**CRAMBOT:** Ha, ha, ha! _____! You think you little _____ scare me? Take this! *(Crambot shoots Snorful with his intergalactic zapper.)*

**SNORFUL:** Oh _____, he shot me. You lousy _____!

**FLOIT:** That's the last _____ straw, Crambot! Die, you _____!

**CRAMBOT & FLOIT:** Aargh! *(Both shoot each other at the same time.)*

# DON'T Say It!

**SCHOOL**
class
building
grade
teacher
bus

**TEST**
quiz
paper
school
class
write

**FRIEND**
pal
buddy
hang out
best
talk

**CHURCH**
building
here
God
Sunday
(your church name)

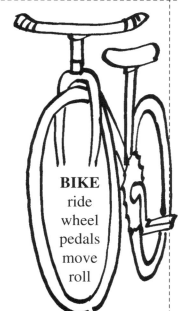

**BIKE**
ride
wheel
pedals
move
roll

**EAT**
food
mouth
drink
taste
chew

**TV**
show
movie
watch
videos
(name of any show)

**MALL**
store
building
shop
food court
(name of any mall)

# OPINIONS

"I try not to swear—I really do. But I'm around it all the time. All of my friends swear like crazy. So I guess I don't think it's a big deal if I slip once in a while"—James, 13

❏ Totally disagree
❏ Kinda disagree
❏ Kinda agree
❏ Totally agree

"I've never sworn—sweared—how do you say that? Anyway, I don't ever swear. I don't think you can call yourself a Christian if you swear"—Tia, 14

❏ Totally disagree
❏ Kinda disagree
❏ Kinda agree
❏ Totally agree

"I just don't see what the big deal is. They're just words—words made of letters. I don't think little alphabet letters put together can really be anything all that wrong"—Karen, 12

❏ Totally disagree
❏ Kinda disagree
❏ Kinda agree
❏ Totally agree

"Give me a pickin' break! If my swearing offends your delicate ears, then don't listen. I think God is big enough to handle any words I could come up with"—Josh, 14

❏ Totally disagree
❏ Kinda disagree
❏ Kinda agree
❏ Totally agree

## Step 1

Play "Mouthwash Tag." Have group members form two teams—"Parents" and "Kids." Instruct both teams to take their places behind a starting line. Give the first "Parent" a bar of soap. The first "Kid" in line will make up a nonsense word and call it out; the first "Parent" should respond, "I'm going to wash your mouth out with soap!" The "Kid" will then try to run to the other side of the room as the "Parent" tries to tag him or her with the bar of soap. Repeat the process with the next "Kid" (who must make up a different nonsense word) and "Parent." Each "Kid" who makes it across the room without being tagged gets a prize; each "Parent" who tags his or her "Kid" gets a prize. Use this activity to introduce the topic of swearing.

## Step 4

Instead of handing out Repro Resource 5, have four kids play the roles on the sheet, reading their "lines" aloud. Other group members should line up behind the readers they most agree with. The catch is that kids must line up behind a reader within fifteen seconds after *that* reader has read, not after all readers have read. If kids wait to line up until after the fourth reader has read, they're stuck with the fourth reader. Afterward, discuss the activity; then let kids change places if they wish.

## Step 1

In a small group, you might want to complete Repro Resource 3 as a mad-lib. In this option, you won't hand out copies of the sheet. Instead, explain that you want group members to provide you with made-up swearwords in various categories that you will provide (noun, verb, name to call someone, and so forth). If you wish, write another "act" of the play so that kids can offer a wider variety of words. You should fill in the blanks as kids respond. When you finish, read aloud the final result.

## Step 2

If you need to, you can adapt the game described in the session for your smaller group. In your version, each person can play against the clock as the rest of the group tries to guess. Keep each person's time (and make sure that everyone really tries to guess when other people are giving the clues). You might also want to add to the examples on Repro Resource 4 to provide two or three opportunities for each group member. Afterward, declare the person with the lowest time to be the winner.

## Step 1

Try another option in place of Repro Resource 3. Before the session, create three different "mad libs" based on hard-boiled dialogue from a TV police drama or from an action-adventure movie. In places where a character might use a swear word or a vulgarity, leave a blank for kids to fill in with the words they come up with while completing the mad lib (e.g., "Put your [adjective] hands behind your head, you [noun], or I'll blow your [adjective] [noun] off"). Have kids form three teams. Give a mad lib to each team. One person on each team will ask for the various kinds of words and then write down group members' suggestions in the appropriate blanks. Group members should *not* know the context of the mad lib while they're suggesting words. After about five minutes, have each team read its completed mad lib.

## Step 4

Ask for volunteers to stand up one at a time and read the statements on Repro Resource 5. After each statement is read, allow the rest of the group members to share whether they agree or disagree with the statement and explain why. You might ask your volunteers to be prepared to defend their statements as though they're the characters on the sheet. (For example, what might might "Josh" say to someone who disagreed with his view of swearing?)

### Step 3

Since swearing is so widespread today, kids may feel that anyone who opposes it is simply living in the past. Keep your side of the discussion as contemporary as possible by using a recent translation of the Bible and explaining ancient-sounding terms like "profanity," "vulgarity," and "filthy language." Before getting too far into the discussion, however, get kids' attention by having an older person from your church (with whom you've arranged this beforehand) walk into your meeting. Walk up to the person and pretend to slap him or her across the face; he or she should reel with the "impact" and stagger out. Ask: **How is swearing like slapping someone in the face?** (It's offensive to many people; using God's name in vain is like slapping Him.)

### Step 5

Kids may be wary of the input-output theory, thinking it implies a "monkey see, monkey do" mentality on their part. In discussing the Matthew passage, emphasize that we need to examine not just our "audio input," but the attitudes in our hearts (out-of-control anger, prejudice, ignoring God) that overflow through our words. Say: **Ken is 14. He keeps finding himself swearing at drivers who get too close when he's riding his bike. What attitudes does he need to work on? Shannara is 13. She says "Oh my God!" whenever she's surprised, then regrets it. What attitudes does she need to work on?**

### Step 3

When you're discussing Exodus 20:7, go through the first four commandments (Exodus 20:1-11) and conduct a short Bible study on *holiness*. Introduce and explain the concept of being "set apart" for God. This comes through strongly in the first two commandments, and is continued in the third one (verse 7). Point out that we frequently dwell on the importance of our actions and attitudes, but we need to remember that our words are just as essential to living as God wants us to live.

### Step 5

Create some tally sheets to hand out to your group members for a research assignment. Across the top of the sheet write the names of the days of the week. Down the left side, write a number of sources from which group members are likely to hear swearing: friends, family, teachers, coaches, TV, movies, and so on. Throughout the week, have kids keep up with how many times they hear swearing from these sources. (They need not write down the words and phrases—just the number of times.) Let them ask questions to clarify what constitutes swearing (heck? dam? pooh?). At your next meeting, point out that the problem may be more widespread and severe than they ever would have expected.

### Step 1

Before the session, set up three areas in your meeting place to serve as stations in an obstacle course. Each station must consist of an obstacle that will require teamwork to work through. Depending on the facilities available to you, these stations could include anything from a four-foot-high bar that everyone must get over without touching to a maze that kids must work through while blindfolded. Be creative! When kids arrive, divide them into three groups. Assign each group to one station. Alter your instructions as appropriate, keeping in mind special needs that any of your kids may have. Emphasize that group members may use only words that encourage each other during the activity. Place an adult at each station to monitor kids' progress. If any discouraging or inappropriate language is used, the entire group must start over. When time is up, ask kids what they thought of the process and how the words of others helped or hindered them. Then say: **As we saw by this activity, negative or cutting words can really set someone back. Today we're going to look at what God thinks of some specific negative words—swear words.**

### Step 5

As you wrap up the session, read Matthew 12:33, 34 again, focusing on the image of the tree. Bring out a large piece of paper on which you've drawn the outline of a tree. At the ends of the branches, have kids write or draw what they think is the good fruit of a Christian life. When they're finished, spend a few minutes thanking and praising God for these good fruits. Then discuss as a group what your kids think the tree (the trunk) should be to produce these good fruits. In other words, what makes a good tree? Fill in the trunk with appropriate answers. Then close in prayer, thanking God again for His goodness.

MOSTLY **GIRLS**

MOSTLY **GUYS**

EXTRA **FUN**

## Step 1

Before the session, you'll need to come up with a list of bizarre but real words and a list of multiple-choice definitions (only one of which is correct) for each word. Instruct your girls to form teams of three or four. One at a time, read aloud the words and their accompanying multiple-choice definitions. The first team to guess the correct definition gets one point. The team with the most points at the end of the game is the winner. Afterward, say: **All words have meaning, whether we think about them much or not. Today we're going to take a look at words that we often hear, but may not think about the effects of— swear words.**

## Step 3

Gather the materials needed to make friendship bracelets (kits are available). After you talk about how swearing might make God feel, ask: **Would you want to speak to your best friend in a way that would make her feel like that?** (No.) **Why?** (I wouldn't want to hurt her. I care about her.) Remind your girls that God is the best friend they could *ever* have. Say: **To help us remember that God is our friend and that He feels hurt when we swear, we're going to make some friendship bracelets. When you wear your bracelet, remember that God wants to be your best friend and think about how He wants you to live.** After your girls have finished their bracelets, encourage them to honor God with both their friendships and their mouths.

## Step 1

After the skit, say: **Suppose that without your knowing it, all of your words and actions yesterday were filmed as a movie. Think carefully. What do you think this movie would be rated? Why? If it were shown to all of your friends and family sitting cozily around the living room TV, would you be at all embarrassed? Why? What would you be willing to do or to pay in order to "edit" the movie before other people saw it?** After your guys respond, ask: **Do you sometimes feel like "real" guys are sort of expected to swear? Why do you think swearing is considered so manly?**

## Step 5

As an ongoing reminder to try to clean up their language, have your guys start a Swearing Fund. Charge 5¢ for each "little" swear and 25¢ for major offenses. Money should be payable at each group meeting. (Make a jar or box available.) Charge double if another group member calls someone on an offense that he hasn't confessed. As guys get better at catching themselves, raise the stakes for offenses. Use the money you accumulate for special refreshments, outings, or some other good cause.

## Step 1

After you've created some swearwords for Repro Resource 3, give kids an opportunity to invent *positive* words. The catch is that the words must incorporate the names of fellow group members. For example, today we speak of brilliant ideas as being Einsteinian because Albert was so smart. And spoonerisms are named for William Spooner, a clergyman who frequently mixed up the initial sounds of his words. Ask your kids to invent positive words and use them in sentences. For example, if John is a guy who makes everyone feel at ease, someone might say, "The Johnnish attention I received when I first came to this group made me feel right at home." If Karen is a boisterous individual, someone might note, "At the concert I went to last night, the performer sang Karenly—loudly and with reckless abandon." After you give a couple of examples, it shouldn't take long for your kids to get the idea and come up with some good new words.

## Step 4

Play "Acceptable Exclamations." Explain that it's almost impossible not to say *something* when you slam your finger in the car door. See how well your kids can do coming up with inoffensive exclamations. Begin with one yourself; then designate a group member to create another one that begins with the last letter of the one you just used. Keep the chain going as long as you can. (For example: ou<u>ch</u>, <u>h</u>oo-we<u>e</u>, <u>e</u>eo<u>w</u>, <u>w</u>owie zowi<u>e</u>, and so forth.) If the chain option is too taxing on the brains of your kids this late in the session, have them select a name to misuse (if they absolutely have to) other than God's. It needs to sound good tripping off the tongue— something like "Mary Poppins!" "Ulysses S. Grant!" or "Tori Spelling!" (You get the idea.)

### Step 2

Play a scene from a video (after pre-screening for appropriateness) in which characters express strong emotions *without* swearing. Then ask: **Would this scene have been better if the character(s) had used swear words? Why or why not? Do you find it hard to express strong emotions without swearing? Why or why not?** Here are some examples of video clips you might use:
• *Searching for Bobby Fischer.* Play the school open-house scene in which the father (Joe Mantegna) lashes out at his son schoolteacher, or a scene in which the chess master (Ben Kingsley) berates Josh, his seven-year-old student.
• *Casablanca.* Show the scene in which Rick (Humphrey Bogart) expresses anger toward Ilsa (Ingrid Bergman) when she walks back into his empty nightclub, or the scene in which Rick angrily tells piano player Sam (Dooley Wilson) to keep playing "As Time Goes By," or the climactic scene in which Rick tells Ilsa why she must get on the plane and forget him.
• *Beethoven.* Show a scene in which the hapless father (Charles Grodin) expresses his frustration over the antics of Beethoven the St. Bernard or over the desire of his family to keep the dog.

### Step 3

Play a contemporary Christian song that honors God's name. Examples might include "Emmanuel" (Amy Grant), "Sing the Glory of His Name" (Stephanie Boosahda), "Oh Holy One" (Debby Boone), "Sing unto Him" (Truth), "You Are Jehovah" (Glen Garrett), "Praise to the King" (Steve Green), "Holy Is His Name" (John Michael Talbot), and "Holy, Holy" (Kathy Troccoli). Then ask: **What names for God are used in this song? Could a person really believe the message of this song and still use God's name in vain? Explain.**

### Step 1

Replace Steps 1 and 2 with a shorter opener. Hand out pages cut from an old book or magazine (look them over beforehand for appropriateness). The pages should be all or mostly text (rather than pictures). Each person gets a page and a pair of scissors. At your signal, each person must cut out at least fifteen words that express an emotion or contain the letter S. But the cutting must be done in a way that keeps the rest of the page in one piece. The person who does so first is the winner. Then ask: **Do you think certain words should be left out of books and magazines? How about movies? Why or why not? If you cut all of the swear words out of your favorite movies, cable TV shows, or novels, would there be much left? Explain.**

### Step 3

To start Step 3, read aloud the four statements from Repro Resource 5 (don't hand it out). Let kids vote on which they most identify with. Then use Step 3 as written. Skip Step 4.

### Step 1

Rather than using Repro Resource 3, have group members brainstorm a list of slang or "street" terms that they've heard recently—words and phrases that *aren't* offensive. See how many your group members can come up with. It's likely that some of your kids will have a hard time coming up with non-offensive or non-swear words. Use this activity to lead in to the questions in the last paragraph of Step 1.

### Step 4

Add the following statement to Repro Resource 5:
• "When I'm with my friends at school or with the guys on the basketball court, I use the language they use. When I'm with my friends at church, I use nicer language. Either way, nobody gets offended, so it's no big deal"—Jerome, 14

**Step 2**
For the "Don't Say It" game on Repro Resource 4, play junior highers versus high schoolers. Add the following cards for your high schoolers: *Car*—drive, gas, license, keys, cruise; *Date*—car, dinner, movie, double, out; *Prom*—dance, music, tuxedo, corsage, senior; *College*—school, graduation, dorm, major, (name of any college).

**Step 4**
Rather than using Repro Resource 5 as is, write out each statement on an index card, omitting the names and ages. Give each card to a volunteer. Instruct the volunteer to read the statement aloud. The rest of the group members may then decide how much or how little they agree with the statement. To jazz things up a bit, you might even want to bring in a supply of costumes and let the volunteers dress for their parts.

**Step 1**
Rather than using Repro Resource 3 with your sixth graders, try a different approach. Have your kids brainstorm a list of "kinda" swear words—words that have the same meanings as swear words or that seem to suggest swear words, but aren't actually swear words. Among the words your kids might name are *gosh, geez, shoot, darn,* and *heck.* After you've got a list of words, ask: **How often are these words used in movies and TV shows?** Your kids will probably recognize that most movies and TV shows don't bother with "kinda" swear words, but instead use the real thing. Discuss the questions in the last paragraph of Step 1; then move on to Step 2.

**Step 5**
Stage a "Garlic Race." Divide kids into teams. Have the members of each team pass with their hands three fresh cloves of garlic, bucket-brigade style, from one side of the room to the other. (If your group is small, have kids keep moving from the beginning to the end of the line so that the passing can continue.) Afterward, have kids smell their hands. The "sweetest-smelling" team wins. Tie this activity into the fact that contact with something—like swearing—can affect us even if we're concentrating on something else.

**Date Used:**

Approx.
Time

**Step 1: Strange
Transmission**  _____
o Extra Action
o Small Group
o Large Group
o Fellowship & Worship
o Mostly Girls
o Mostly Guys
o Extra Fun
o Short Meeting Time
o Urban
o Sixth Grade
Things needed:

**Step 2: Don't Say It!**  _____
o Small Group
o Media
o Combined Junior High/High School
Things needed:

**Step 3: Squeaky Clean**  _____
o Heard It All Before
o Little Bible Background
o Mostly Girls
o Media
o Short Meeting Time
Things needed:

**Step 4: A Difference of
Opinions**  _____
o Extra Action
o Large Group
o Extra Fun
o Urban
o Combined Junior High/High School
Things needed:

**Step 5: Input-Output**  _____
o Heard It All Before
o Little Bible Background
o Fellowship & Worship
o Mostly Guys
o Sixth Grade
Things needed:

# 3 "If You Can't Say Something Nice . . ."

## YOUR GOALS FOR THIS SESSION:

*Choose one or more*

☐ To help kids recognize the effects that put-downs have on people.

☐ To help kids understand why putting others down is a bad habit.

☐ To help kids practice saying encouraging things to other people.

☐ Other _____

**Your Bible Base:**

Proverbs 18:6, 7
1 Thessalonians 5:11, 15

# The Average Junior Higher

*(Needed: Large sheets of paper, markers, masking tape, scissors)*

Have kids form groups of four. Give each group a large sheet of paper (approximately six feet long) and markers. Instruct each group to draw a life-size "average" junior higher. The junior higher may be a guy or a girl. You might suggest that each group trace an outline of one of its members' bodies to get started. (However, make sure group members don't get marker all over the clothes of the person they're tracing.) After about five minutes, have each group cut out its drawing and tape it to the front wall of your meeting area.

Ask: **How many of you heard someone get put down this week?**
**How many of you got put down this week?**
**How many of you put down someone else this week?**

After getting a show of hands for each question, say: **Let's pretend that the "average" junior highers you drew are real junior highers. Who's willing to try out a put-down on one of them?** Have volunteers come forward one at a time and put down (verbally) one of the paper junior highers. After a put down is delivered, have the volunteer tear off a portion of the "recipient" (a full limb would be an appropriate amount).

Once this activity gets going, you'll probably have plenty of volunteers, as kids will want to rip pieces off drawings other than their own. When the paper junior highers are looking fairly tattered, stop the activity.

Ask: **How do these junior highers look now? How is what we just did kind of like real life?** (When we put people down, we destroy them—even if it's only a little at a time.)

**STEP**
**2**

# The 3 P's of Verbal Ripping

*(Needed: Bibles, copies of Repro Resource 6, pencils, chalkboard and chalk or newsprint and marker)*

Ask: **Why do you think junior highers get into put-downs so much?** (To make themselves feel superior to others; because someone's bugging them and they want that person to know it; to get attention from others; because someone ripped on them.)

**Why do you think God cares if we put others down?** Don't correct group members' responses here—just let them throw out any ideas they have.

Hand out copies of "The 3 P's of Verbal Ripping" (Repro Resource 6) and pencils. Explain to your group members that they're going to look at what the Bible has to say about three questions: "Why not rip?" "How should we respond to rip attacks?" and "What's a better plan?"

Write the numbers 1, 2 and 3 down the left side of the board. Write a capital "P" next to each number.

Refer to the first question on your group members' sheets. Have everyone look up Proverbs 18:6, 7. Have someone read the passage aloud. This passage talks about some of the personal consequences of foolish talk (including put-downs). Next to the first "P" on the board, write "Put-downs bring trouble." Have your group members write the same thing on their sheets.

Then ask: **What might be some of the negative results if you put people down all the time?** (Loss of friends, loneliness, having people put you down all the time.)

Move on to the second question on your group members' sheets. Have everyone look up I Thessalonians 5:15. While kids are looking it up, remind them that you're looking for an answer to the "How to respond" question. Have someone read aloud the verse. Then write "Paybacks are dumb" next to the second "P" on the board. Have group members write the same thing on their sheets.

Ask: **If someone puts you down and you pay them back by putting them down, what will probably happen next?** (More put-downs.)

**Have you ever been in a situation in which you and some-one else put each other down all the time?** Many of your group members will probably admit that they have. **If so, how did the situation finally end?** (In most cases, it either doesn't end or it

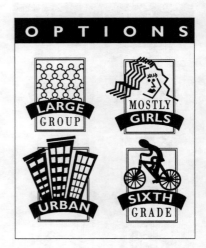

**O P T I O N S**

LARGE GROUP

MOSTLY GIRLS

URBAN

SIXTH GRADE

escalates into more serious problems. Sometimes the relationship can just fade away into silence—ignoring each other.)

Move on to the third question on your group members' sheets. Have kids look back a few verses in their Bibles to I Thessalonians 5:11. Remind them that you're looking for "a better plan." Ask someone to read aloud the verse. Then write "Promote others" next to the third "P" on the board. Have group members write the same thing on their sheets.

Ask: **What does it mean to promote others?** (To build people up, to say good things about them.)

Before you move on to the next step, review all three questions and the "P" statements that answer them.

STEP
3

# Promotion Plan

*(Needed: Copies of Repro Resource 7, pencils, copies of the skit dialogue)*

Say: **Let's pretend we've all decided we're never going to put someone down again! All we're going to do is the third "P"—promote people. There's only one small problem. How do we do this without sounding like a total idiot?**

Hand out copies of the dialogue in the following three situations to six group members (two group members per situation). Have the actors perform the brief dialogues in front of the group.

*Situation 1*
STUDENT A: You really are a worthless piece of filth.
STUDENT B: I really value you. You're such a special person!

*Situation 2*
STUDENT A *(standing alone)*: I hope I can find someone to eat with at lunch.
STUDENT B *(approaching)*: Hello. You're God's special creation, and I appreciate you!

*Situation 3*
STUDENT A: So, did you finish your homework?
STUDENT B: What a special question! You have such good communication skills!

Ask: **What's wrong with these situations? Is that how you think God wants us to act? Why or why not?**

After you get a few responses, hand put copies of "Promotion Plan" (Repro Resource 7). Say: **Here's what we're going to do. First, write down the names of three people you'd really enjoy putting down. These people might be your best friends or they might be people who really bug you. They might even be family members.**

Give kids a minute or two to work. Then say: **Now spend a couple of minutes writing things you could say or do to promote that person without making you sound like a total idiot.**

After a few minutes, have volunteers share their ideas with the rest of the group. However, don't force anyone to share who doesn't want to.

# The Put-Up Contest

Have kids form two teams. Instruct each team to choose two representatives to compete in a contest. Have the two contestants from one team stand facing the two from the other team, about five feet apart. Explain that you're going to have a "put-up" contest, which is the opposite of a put-down contest. Announce that each team will have ten seconds to say something positive about one of the contestants from the other team. Emphasize that all "put-ups" must be phrased in the form of a put-down. They must all start with the words "Oh yeah, well . . ."

The two contestants on a team will alternate turns for their team; but when one gets eliminated, the other must go it alone. Players are eliminated when they can't think of anything to say within ten seconds or when they repeat a "put-up" that has already been given by someone else.

Point to one of the contestants and say, **Go.** After he or she gives a "put-up," point to a contestant on the other team. Continue back and forth, pausing only to eliminate players. At the end of the game, have everyone cheer for the winner.

Close the session in prayer, asking God to help your group members (1) avoid putting down others, (2) learn how to respond properly when others put them down, and (3) learn how to promote people.

# THE 3 P'S OF VERBAL RIPPING

## 1. Why Not Rip?
*(Proverbs 18:6, 7)*

*P*

## 2. How Should We Respond to Rip Attacks?
*(I Thessalonians 5:15)*

P

## 3. What's a Better Plan?
*(I Thessalonians 5:11)*

# PROMOTION PLAN

**People I'd Like to Rip**

**Promotion Plan**

1.

2.

3.

## Step 3

Bring in a supply of bricks or concrete blocks. Have kids form two teams. Give half of the bricks or blocks to each team. As you discuss Repro Resource 7, each team should build three steps and label them with the "P's," using stick-on labels and markers. Give a prize to the team whose steps do the best job of "lifting you up" (without falling apart) when you try a "test walk" on them.

## Step 4

Bring a supply of trite, flowery, sentimental greeting cards that gush about how wonderful the receiver is. Give each person a card. At your signal, kids should trade their cards with each other, with each person trying to end up with a less phony-sounding one than he or she started with. Kids must trade the cards they're holding every ten seconds. Stop the game without warning after about a minute. Discuss kids' opinions of the cards they hold. Then have kids rewrite the cards they're holding to make them sound complimentary, but more "real."

## Step 1

Rather than using paper outlines, have your kids stand against the wall. Explain that you will play the role of a fellow student inviting them to visit your youth group for the first time. Then do so, but in a way that ignores their concerns and puts them down in some way. Instruct kids to stand until they decide for sure not to come. Then they should sit. You might use the following statements:

• **Please come to our group. We never have many people, so it's pretty dull.**
• **At our group, you don't have to be smart or talented.**
• **If you can't find anything better to do tonight, join the rest of us who can't either.**

Help your kids see that such invitations are essentially saying, "You should come to our youth group tonight. We've got a lot of other losers there, so you'll feel right at home." Though low-key and subtle, these invitations are put-downs all the same. Challenge kids to be more alert to how put-downs can relate to spiritual matters (and perhaps even the low number of people who attend the group).

## Step 4

As you wrap up the session, ask: **What if we built up everyone the way we've just done for each other? Do you think the size of our group would change? If so, why? Do you think the closeness of the group would change? If so, in what ways?** Try to provide a vision of better unity and perhaps numerical growth for your group in the future.

## Step 1

Before you begin the poster-tearing exercise, use another activity to introduce the topic of putting others down. You'll need a couple of foreign language dictionaries. Explain to your group members that you will read a word or phrase in another language. If kids believe that the word or phrase is a put-down, they should remain seated; if they believe the word or phrase is not a put-down, they should stand up. Read several words and phrases, pausing after each one to give kids an opportunity to respond. Then reveal what the word or phrase actually means.

## Step 2

Have kids form teams of four or five. Hand out paper and pencils to each team. Give the teams two minutes to write down as many put-downs that a junior higher might hear as they can think of. After two minutes, see which team has the longest list. Then ask: **Why do you think junior highers get into put-downs so much?** Continue through Step 2.

## Step 3

Kids may have heard many times that they aren't supposed to put each other down. But unless the underlying causes of put-downs are dealt with, the "ripping" probably will continue. Along with the "three P's," talk about "three I's" that cause put-downs. *Insecurity*, the feeling that we aren't good enough or cool enough, can lead us to tear "the competition" down so that we feel strong or important. *Impatience* can cause us to lash out at others when things aren't going our way. *Insensitivity* causes us to forget how much our "funny" put-downs can hurt others. A healthy relationship with God can develop the opposites of these "three I's" in our lives—confidence, patience, and compassion. Ask: **How did Jesus demonstrate confidence, patience, and compassion when He could have used put-downs instead?** (Examples might include when the soldiers came to get Him in Gethsemane; at His trial; and on the cross.)

## Step 4

Forced compliments may serve a purpose, but jaded kids—whether givers or receivers—won't put much stock in them. Try another option instead. Before the session, buy reward stickers—the kind teachers and parents use to affirm kids. These stickers, which bear "put-ups" like "Way to Go!" and "You're Number One!" are available at card shops, discount stores, and educational supply stores. To close the meeting, give each person at least half a dozen stickers. Say: **Put these stickers in your pocket, wallet, or purse. During the next forty-eight hours, stick them on at least three people who deserve them—three people outside of this group. Try to catch those people doing something right.**

## Step 3

A group without much Bible knowledge may not realize why put-downs are so destructive. Ask a couple of volunteers to do an impromptu skit of Adam and Eve in the Garden of Eden as it might have been if they'd begun to put down one another. This skit should show how a couple of people who refuse to get along can destroy even the most perfect relationship that God can create. It may also be that your group of kids has not had the teachings about self-image that are frequent in other groups. You may need to spend some time explaining that if we truly believe that each individual is created in the image of God and is special to Him, and if we need each other in order to function as a "body," then put-downs cannot be tolerated.

## Step 4

The "put-up" contest may be "too little too late" if your kids have never experienced the reality of God's love. While they will hear positive comments for a couple of minutes during this step, that will hardly cancel out a lifetime of put-downs, if such has been the case. So after kids have heard from their secular friends, and after they've heard from fellow youth group members, let them hear from a higher authority. Explain that you want them to see how God feels about them—no matter what other people might say. Start by having them examine passages such as Psalm 139; John 3:16-18; Romans 8:35-39; and any other passages that you think are appropriate to give kids a better understanding of their value to God—and what *should* be their value to others.

## Step 1

Before the session, create a set of name tags, half of which have positive messages such as "Hug me" or "Give me a compliment" and half of which have negative messages such as "Kick me" or "Tweak my nose." Make sure that you have at least one name tag for every member of your group. As group members arrive, stick a name tag on each person's back, making sure that no one sees his or her own tag. Play some fun, upbeat music. Encourage kids to mingle around the room, checking out each other's name tags and responding accordingly. However, make sure that no one gets carried away in responding to a name tag instruction. After a few minutes, ask: **What did you think of this activity?** Answers will vary, depending on the name tags kids had. Point out that put-downs are a lot like this activity. If you continue to get swift kicks, pretty soon you start to expect them, and either develop defenses or start to avoid people—both of which lead to loneliness and alienation.

## Step 4

Write the following on the board: "A—Adoration; C—Confession; T—Thanksgiving; S—Supplication." Briefly explain that these steps are a prayer guide—"A" involves offering praise to God for the wonderful things He is; "C" involves confessing our sins; "T" involves thanking God for what He's done; and "S" involves offering our requests to God. Give your kids an opportunity to put the ACTS method to use—adoring God for being an encourager to them, confessing times when they've put someone down recently, thanking God for giving them the strength to build others up, and making supplication for a week filled with "put-ups."

MOSTLY GIRLS

MOSTLY GUYS

EXTRA FUN

## Step 2

Put-downs are something that most junior high girls deal with every day—probably more so than guys. You may want to supplement your discussion with the following questions: **Do you think girls are more prone to putting others down than guys are? Why or why not?** (Girls learn at an early age that the tongue is an effective weapon. Many guys learn to rely on their fists.) **Why do you put others down?** (Often the reason we put others down is to make up for an area in ourselves in which we feel inferior.) Depending on the closeness of your group, your girls may or may not be willing to answer this question. **What steps can you take to change your attitude so that you'll not be so likely to put others down?** If nothing else, this question may get your group members thinking about their attitude.

## Step 4

Before your girls begin the "put-up" contest, ask for a volunteer. Have the volunteer sit on a stool at the front of the room. Announce that you're going to give her a make-over. As you begin to apply the makeup, gush on and on about how beautiful she is and how ravishing she'll be when you're finished—really lay it on thick. Then proceed to lay the makeup on thick—very thick. After you've made a real mess of her face, turn to the group and ask: **So what do you think of my encouraging words? Don't you think she feels great about herself now?** (Obviously not.) Point out that our words must be sincere and truthful in order to be of any value.

## Step 1

Begin the session by letting group members create some skits. One group should do a skit on "How my world would be different if my *friends* were always positive." Another group should do a skit on "How my world would be different if my *coach* were always positive." Other groups might try to envision ever-positive teachers, parents, bosses, and other influences in their lives. The forced focus on being positive will probably do much to remind your guys of how much negative influence they regularly have to deal with.

## Step 4

Guys traditionally aren't comfortable with verbal encouragement. So rather than using the "put-up" contest, you might want to let them work on improving their *nonverbal* methods of affirmation. ("Nonverbal" doesn't necessarily mean "silent.") Have each guy act out a way to affirm someone else that doesn't require words. For example, guys might shake hands, give a pat on the back, do a high five, buy someone a soft drink, give a good-natured punch on the arm, or whatever. Perhaps your group members might even invent a *new* method of showing admiration or affection for each other that will be special to them from now on.

## Step 3

Wrap up this step by playing and discussing the Randy Newman song "Short People." Let kids discuss why they think the writer wrote the song. (Is he really putting down short people or is he making a statement about our prejudices in general?) Encourage kids to think of other groups of people who are frequently ridiculed. They might do well to think in terms of "humor": Polish jokes, blonde jokes, lawyer jokes, and so forth. Ask: **Why do you think people stereotype and put down entire groups of people?** If kids can think of any groups *they* are guilty of putting down in the past, have them select one of the groups and write a positive song about those people. (Kids who can't think of specific groups can help out others who do.) When they finish, let kids sing their positive songs with all of the gusto they can muster.

## Step 4

"Saturday Night Live" frequently invents characters who have a lot of personality: Cajun Man, Opera Man, Mr. Short-Term Memory, and others. Let your group members create "Mr. (or Mrs.) Positive," who remains upbeat in spite of all of the put-downs he or she receives. Let your kids first write out some of the harshest put-downs they have recently received. Then use them against Mr. (or Mrs.) Positive to see how he or she responds. For example, one might person say, "Mr. (or Mrs.) Positive, I hear you studied all night and still couldn't pass your urine test"—to which Mr. (or Mrs.) Positive might reply, "What a witty remark! Did you hear it somewhere, or did your own inventive mind think it up?" By witnessing the always-positive nature of Mr. (or Mrs.) Positive, your kids might exercise a bit of additional strength the next time they are verbally accosted by someone.

### Step 1

Bring in a loaded video camera. Have kids stand or sit wherever they want to in your meeting place. Tell kids that you're going to work your way through the group with the camera on, giving kids a chance to hurl their best put-downs at the camera. Then do so. After bearing the brunt of kids' insults, have the group sit. Explain that you were using a "Victim-Cam"—and what you're about to play back shows what it's like to be on the receiving end of put-downs. Play back the tape and discuss the fact that most of us don't think of the victim's perspective when we're using "clever" put-downs.

### Step 4

Play one or two clips from a motivational tape—audio or video. This kind of tape is designed to "pump up" the listener's or viewer's self-esteem, usually to improve emotional health or to increase effectiveness as a salesperson. If you can't borrow such a tape from a salesperson in your church, go to a bookstore and look for tapes by speakers like Zig Ziglar, Og Mandino, Earl Nightengale, or Les Brown. Or check the "Community Service" or "Self-Help" section of a video rental store to find a motivational tape designed for teenagers—on a subject like staying off drugs or how to study. After playing one or two appropriate segments, ask: **How was this the opposite of a put-down? How did the speaker(s) try to "promote" you? How could you get the same message across, but in your own words?**

### Step 1

Replace Steps 1 and 2 with a shorter opener. Bring photos of yourself (ask a helper to take several Polaroid shots of you before the session). Have kids form teams of two to four. Give each team a photo and a laundry marker. Have the teams compete for one minute to see who can make your photo look most stupid— adding goofy hair, bow ties, zits, big ears, etc. Award prizes, if you like. Then ask: **How are put-downs designed to make people look stupid? How would you feel if we'd used your picture in this contest? What does that tell you about what it's like to be the target of put-downs?**

### Step 3

Use Repro Resource 6 for your own reference as you lead the "three P's" discussion, but don't take time to hand it out or to have kids write notes on it. In Step 3, ask kids to think of positive things to say about just one person rather than three. In Step 4, simplify the contest by giving each team one minute to come up with a single cheer that promotes the other team. If you like, give a prize for enthusiastic delivery, sincerity, or choice of words.

### Step 1

Spend some time talking about "the dozens," a popular street game in which the sole purpose is to insult your opponent as badly (and as humorously) as possible. Ask: **How do you think this game got started? Why is it sometimes fun to put down other people? How damaging do you think a game like that is? Why?**

### Step 2

To illustrate the first "P" ("Put-downs bring trouble") on Repro Resource 6, ask group members to share some examples of put-down exchanges that escalated into more serious confrontations and perhaps even resulted in violence. If possible, be prepared to share an example of your own. Ask: **How do you know if a person will respond jokingly to a put-down or whether he or she will be offended and angered by it?** (You *don't* know—that's the point. What you might think is a harmless, good-natured put-down may be offensive to the person you're putting down.)

**PLANNING CHECKLIST**

**Step 1**
Divide your kids into groups of four, making sure that you get an even distribution of junior highers and high schoolers in each group. Hand out large sheets of paper and markers. Instruct group members to create a life-sized "average" teenager (rather than specifically a junior higher). Add the following questions to your discussion of the activity: **Of the people you put down this week, what percent would you say were older than you? What percent would you say were your age? What percent would you say were younger than you?** Some of your high schoolers may think this entire session is beneath them. If so, ask them how often they hear adults putting one another down. Remind them that this is a problem that some people struggle with all of their lives.

**Step 4**
Instead of using the "put-up" contest (in which you could pit your junior highers against your high schoolers, if you wish), go back to the situations presented in Step 3. Choose one junior higher and one high schooler for each roleplay. Set up the situations, using the same dialogue for Student A. However, this time, have Student B respond in a more realistic—but still positive—manner. You may wish to point out that sometimes the best response is to just walk away. After you've completed each situation, discuss as a group how it was handled and what your group members could do when they face similar situations.

**Step 2**
As you work through the three "P's" on Repro Resource 6, hold your discussion on the front steps or inside stairs of your meeting place. Have kids sit on the steps as you talk. After each point, your group members should move up a step. Tie this in to the fact that the three "steps" on Repro Resource 6 lift people up rather than bringing them down.

**Step 3**
Rather than having your sixth graders perform the three dialogues in Step 3, try a different approach. Ask: **How can you tell when someone's being fake or insincere in "promoting" another person?** Let group members list several ways to spot a fake. Then ask: **What do you do when you suspect that someone is giving you a fake compliment? How do you feel about people who "fake" promoting other people? Why?** Hand out copies of Repro Resource 7. In the second part of the instructions for the sheet, say: **Now spend a couple of minutes writing things you could say or do to promote that person without making you sound like a total *fake*.**

**Date Used:**

Approx.
Time

**Step 1: The Average
Junior Higher** _____
o Small Group
o Large Group
o Fellowship & Worship
o Mostly Guys
o Media
o Short Meeting Time
o Urban
o Combined Junior High/High School
Things needed:

**Step 2: The 3 P's of
Verbal Ripping** _____
o Large Group
o Mostly Girls
o Urban
o Sixth Grade
Things needed:

**Step 3: Promotion Plan** _____
o Extra Action
o Heard It All Before
o Little Bible Background
o Extra Fun
o Short Meeting Time
o Sixth Grade
Things needed:

**Step 4: The Put-Up
Contest** _____
o Extra Action
o Small Group
o Heard It All Before
o Little Bible Background
o Fellowship & Worship
o Mostly Girls
o Mostly Guys
o Extra Fun
o Media
o Combined Junior High/High School
Things needed:

# Did You Hear about . . . ?

## YOUR GOALS FOR THIS SESSION:

*Choose one or more*

☐ To help kids recognize what gossip is.

☐ To help kids understand how destructive gossip is.

☐ To help kids begin to practice "anti-gossip," saying something good about someone else.

☐ Other _____

_____

## Your Bible Base:

Romans 1:29, 30
James 3:3-6

PROVERBS: 11:13
16:28
18:8
26:20

O P T I O N S

STEP
1

# Say What?

Begin the session with a storytelling activity. Have kids sit in a circle. Explain to your group members that they're going to tell a story—but that they'll have only pieces of the story to work with.

Begin the story as follows: **This guy named Bill was walking home from school one day . . .** Then explain that the person with the longest hair in the group should add a sentence to the story by whispering it to the person on his or her left. That person should then add a sentence to the story and whisper the whole thing to the person on his or her left. Keep going all the way around the circle. Strongly urge your kids (especially the guys) to keep the story clean. Once the last person has heard the story, he or she should think of a final sentence to add. That person should then tell the entire story to the group.

Afterward, ask: **Isn't that how gossip works? The story starts one way and gets changed or added to along its path. The result is often not even true—that's part of the reason the Bible tells us to ignore gossip.**

O P T I O N S

STEP
2

# Gossip Gus

*(Needed: Copy of Repro Resource 8)*

Ask for six volunteers to act out the skit on "Gossip Gus" (Repro Resource 8). If you have a small group, you may either double up on parts or eliminate some of the characters in the skit. Give a copy of the script only to the narrator of the skit. After you've assigned all of the roles, explain that your actors will be taking part in a "spontaneous melodrama." The narrator will read the story and the actors must act it out as they hear the lines. They should repeat all of the dialogue lines the narrator gives them with as much energy and excitement as they can muster. Encourage the actors to really "ham it up." Encourage the audience to enter into the action like a melodrama audience should— with cheers, hisses, sighs, and other reactions. Afterward, give a big round of applause to your performers.

# Big Results

*(Needed: Bibles, copies of Repro Resource 9, pencils)*

Hand out copies of "Small Stuff, Big Results" (Repro Resource 9) and pencils. Say: **We're going to look at some really small things that have big-time results.**

Instruct group members to look at the first box on the sheet. Explain: **A spark is a tiny, tiny thing. But it can start a fire that can destroy an entire forest.**

Move on to the second box. Explain: **A ship's rudder is certainly bigger than a spark, but it's pretty small compared to the whole ship. Yet the rudder controls the direction of even the largest vessels.**

Give group members a couple of minutes to think of other examples of small things that produce big results. Instruct them to draw pictures of their ideas in boxes 3 and 4. After a few minutes, have group members display and explain their pictures. Examples might include things like one grain of sand in an oyster being made into a big, beautiful pearl; one little blockage in an artery causing a heart attack that can kill someone; one final straw breaking a camel's back; and one little finger on a trigger ending someone's life.

Then refer your group members to the fifth box on the sheet, which has "James 3:3-6" in it. Ask group members to look up the passage in their Bibles. Have one of them read it aloud. The passage talks about the mighty destructive power of the tongue—comparing it to a ship's rudder and a spark starting a forest fire.

Ask: **Have you ever been hurt by someone's gossiping about you? If so, what happened?**

**How is it that something so small as our tongue can do so much damage?** If no one mentions it, point out that the "tongue" is just a way of referring to talking.

**What are some of the negative effects of gossip?** (Losing friends, hurting people, etc.)

**Why do people gossip?** (To hear juicy stories, to make themselves seem cool, etc.)

**Why do you think gossip is so much more common among junior highers than among fourth and fifth graders?** (Perhaps because junior highers care a lot more about what people think of them.)

Refer your group members to Box 6 on Repro Resource 9. Instruct them to draw in the box a person's face with a tongue coming out of the person's mouth. Instruct kids not to draw the tongue according to its normal size, but a size that more accurately reflects its destructive power. After a minute or two, allow volunteers to show their pictures to the rest of the group.

Have someone read aloud Romans 1:29, 30. Then ask: **Did you hear "gossip" in the middle of all that? Why do you think God would include gossip with all of that really wicked stuff?** (God must think gossip is really wicked.)

# What's Gossip?

*(Needed: Copies of Repro Resource 10, pencils)*

Say: **OK, we know gossip is a really destructive force that can do lots of damage. We also know that gossip displeases God. But some of you might not really be sure about what exactly gossip is.**

Hand out copies of "What's Gossip?" (Repro Resource 10). Instruct group members to write a definition of gossip in the first blank space. After about a minute, have a few volunteers share their definitions. Then give kids the following definition: **Gossip is talking about people in destructive ways when they aren't around.**

Lead group members through the eight examples on the sheet one at a time. Read each example aloud; then pause long enough for group members to write down whether they think the situation involves gossip or not. When kids are finished, ask them to share their responses. Use the following suggested answers to supplement your discussion of the sheet: 1—gossip; 2—gossip; 3—not gossip (but not nice); 4—not gossip; 5—gossip; 6—gossip; 7—not gossip; 8—gossip.

OPTIONS

SMALL GROUP

LARGE GROUP

EXTRA FUN

MEDIA

URBAN

JR. HIGH / HIGH SCHOOL COMBINED

SIXTH GRADE

# Anti-Gossip

Say: **Now that we're a little clearer on what gossip is, let me ask you this question: "What's the opposite of gossip?"** (Saying positive things about someone when they're not around.)

Continue: **We're going to try this right now. It might seem a little weird—all right, it might seem really weird! But that's only because most of us don't do it very often.**

Ask group members to think of something positive they can say about someone in the room. After about thirty seconds, have everyone find someone to share his or her positive statement with (but it may *not* be the person the positive statement is about). Make sure you participate in this activity as well.

Close the session in prayer, asking God to help your group members break habits of gossiping and to give them the courage not to listen to gossip.

# GOSSIP GUS

*Characters:* Narrator; Gossip Gus; Gus' friends—Bert, Orville, and Thurman; Prudence, the girl Gus likes

Our story takes place in the hallways of Stoobleville Public Junior High School. When we first see Gus, he's walking down Hall B with his friend Bert. "Gossip Gus," as people call him, is busy at work trying to be cool by talking about other people.

"Hey, Bert," says Gus.

"Yeah?" responds Bert.

"Did ya hear about Orville and Prudence?"

Just then, Orville walks up behind Gus and Bert and smacks them on the back. "Hi, guys," he says.

"Hey, Orville," say Bert and Gus in perfect unison.

Orville asks, "What were you saying about me and Prudence?"

Gus quickly says, "Oh, nothing." He looks down and shuffles his feet to buy some time.

Bert says, "Yeah, Gus, you were saying something about Prudence and . . ."

Before he can finish his sentence, Gus slaps his hand over Bert's mouth and says, "Prudence and Thurman—I asked if you'd heard the news about Prudence and Thurman."

Just then, Thurman walks up behind them all, smacks them all on the back and says, "Hi, guys!"

"Hey, Thurman," they all say in perfect unison.

Thurman looks at Gus and asks, "What about me and Prudence?"

"Nothing," says Gus calmly, looking up in the air to buy time.

Bert speaks up, "Yeah, Gus, you were saying something about Prudence and . . ." Gus slaps his hand over Bert's mouth and quickly says, "Prudence and some guy from Horkdale Middle School. I said, 'Did you hear the news about Prudence and some guy from Horkdale Middle School?'"

Just then Prudence walks up from the side. She says, "Hey, guys" and slaps Gus on the face.

The other guys are really excited that no one slapped them on the back. They all say, "Hey, Prudence," in perfect unison.

Prudence throws Gus against the wall and pins him there by holding her finger in the middle of his chest.

"Gus," she says, "I'd go out with any of your friends before I'd go out with a gossip like you!"

Prudence, Bert, Orville, and Thurman all walk away together arm-in-arm. And Gus is left alone without anything or anyone.

The end.

# Small Stuff
# Big Results

**1**

**2**

**3**

**4**

**5**

James 3:3-6

**6**

# WHAT'S GOSSIP?

*My definition:*

**1.** Mary calls Meg to tell her that Bobby just broke up with Francine—which is true.
- ❏ Gossip    ❏ Not Gossip

**2.** Terrance tells Andre and Justin that he heard that Jill will make out with any guy who takes her out.
- ❏ Gossip    ❏ Not Gossip

**3.** Teresa's at lunch with Fran and Stacie. She tells Stacie that Fran got a bad grade on her test.
- ❏ Gossip    ❏ Not Gossip

**4.** Anthony tells Phil that he's really mad at him.
- ❏ Gossip    ❏ Not Gossip

**5.** Connie tells Tom that Suzie likes him. Suzie's never said anything about Tom to Connie.
- ❏ Gossip    ❏ Not Gossip

**6.** Jason tells Ben that Dave told him that Derrick said he "went all the way" with Melanie.
- ❏ Gossip    ❏ Not Gossip

**7.** Bernice tells Shawna how much the card she got from Laura meant to her.
- ❏ Gossip    ❏ Not Gossip

**8.** Jen tells Jeannie that Amy said that Tiffany said that Anita said that Penny said that Kathy said that Debbie wants to run away.
- ❏ Gossip    ❏ Not Gossip

## Step 1

Instead of using the storytelling activity, have kids form two teams. Instruct each team to stand in a line, one person behind another, all facing the same direction. Tape a sheet of paper to each person's back. Give each person a crayon. Show the last person in each line a simple picture (barn, dog, fish, etc.). At your signal, that person will silently try to draw the same kind of picture on the paper taped to the person in front of him or her. That person, also silent, will try to feel what's being drawn on his or her back and attempt to draw the same thing on the paper taped to the next person. The process continues down the line. The first team to complete the process wins. Afterward, display each team's pictures in order. Discuss how the picture changed as it got further from the "source." Use this activity to illustrate how the truth can get more and more distorted as it's heard secondhand, thirdhand, etc.

## Step 3

Replace Repro Resource 9 with a "Tongue Talent Show." Let each person choose to either (1) dial a phone number with his or her tongue (put a new piece of plastic wrap over the phone before each attempt), or (2) make a star design with five toothpicks in twenty seconds, using only his or her tongue. Tie this activity into the "power" of the tongue.

## Step 1

Instead of using the opening activity, begin the session by surreptitiously calling everyone to one corner of the room. Start talking about people in and out of the group. Everything you say should be the absolute truth, but you should act as if you're clueing kids in on big juicy secrets. For example, you might say: **Pssst! Did you hear about Pastor Smith? I saw him out for a late-night walk with some woman last night. I don't need to say any more, do I?** Wink knowingly, not bothering to mention that the woman was his wife of twenty-three years. Afterward, ask: **Why do people seem to take such joy in sharing secrets and spreading gossip? Have you ever been guilty of spreading gossip? Have you ever been a victim of someone else's gossip?**

## Step 4

After kids complete Repro Resource 10, ask: **What's the potential effect of gossip on a small group like ours?** Help kids see the benefit of more intimate relationships that are possible in small groups, but warn them of the accompanying drawback of possibly having confidential information shared by group members at school as gossip. Read a number of statements to see how your kids feel about gossip. If kids agree with a statement, they should stand; if they disagree, they should sit. Make a list of your own, but here are a few statements to get you started:
• **I hold back facts about myself in this group because I'm afraid that people might use the information against me later on.**
• **I have passed along information shared in confidence in this group to other people outside the group— not often, but sometimes.**
• **I think more people would attend this group if they weren't afraid of gossip.**

## Step 1

If you don't think the storytelling activity would work well with your group, try another option. Ask for several volunteers to compete in a word game. On the board, write the word "cat." One at a time, have your contestants change, add, or subtract one letter in the word to make a new word. For instance, "cat" might become "bat," which might become "bait," which might become "bit," and so on. If a contestant can't come up with a new word in ten seconds, he or she is out. Continue until only one person remains. Afterward, point out that gossip is similar to the words in the game—it starts out one way and gets changed or added to along its path.

## Step 4

After deciding which situations on Repro Resource 10 involve gossip, have kids form five teams. Assign each team one of the gossip situations (1, 2, 5, 6, 8) from the sheet. Instruct each team to come up with a scenario that describes what might happen to the person being gossiped about as a result of the gossip. For instance, for #2, how might some of the guys at school start treating Jill as a result of Terrance's gossip? After a few minutes, have each team share its scenario.

## HEARD IT ALL BEFORE

### Step 1

If kids associate the word "gossip" with chattering housewives at backyard fences, they may assume that this session doesn't relate to them and tune out. Use the following to illustrate that all of us have opportunities to gossip, whether or not we call it that. (1) **You've heard a couple of kids speculate that your music teacher is gay. Is there anyone in the world you would repeat that rumor to? Why?** (2) **A friend has just turned his back on you and joined a "cooler" group that rejects you. Another friend of yours says to forget your former friend, who is "a jerk." You happen to know the former friend is so afraid of the dark that he still sleeps with a light on. Do you mention it? Why or why not?** (3) **A new kid shows up at the youth group. You once heard someone at school say that the kid is HIV-positive. What do you do?**

### Step 5

If you used the "say something nice about each other" activity in Session 3, try another option. Have the group brainstorm a list of the "Top Five Gossip Stoppers." These would be phrases kids could use to re-route a conversation that's heading into gossipy territory. Examples might include: "Just the facts, ma'am"; "No comment"; "Can I quote you on that?" and "Please speak into the microphone." Then have kids compete to see who can say the phrases most politely, in a way that would steer a conversation in the right direction without cutting it off.

## LITTLE BIBLE BACKGROUND

### Step 3

Prior to reading Romans 1:29, 30, announce that you want group members to play "Rate-a-Sin." Explain that you will read a list of sins. After each one, kids should rate it on a scale of one (least) to ten (most) according to how "bad" it is. Then read the list, one item at a time, from Romans 1:29, 30—without letting on that it's a biblical list. See how gossip compares to some of the other things. If it's rated lower, as it might well be, read the passage aloud and emphasize that gossip is just as bad as anything else on the list.

### Step 5

If your group members suddenly come to the conclusion that gossip is not something that "everybody does" and not even just a bad habit, but rather a serious sin, they may begin to feel a lot of guilt for past actions. Close with a silent prayer of confession and repentance. Assure kids that God forgives those who sincerely repent. Also challenge your kids to take the additional step of seeking forgiveness from people they may have offended in the past.

## FELLOWSHIP & WORSHIP

### Step 1

Write the words to a story—perhaps a favorite children's story, a Bible story, or the lyrics to a popular song—on slips of paper, one or two lines per slip. Put each slip inside a balloon; inflate the balloon. Make sure that you have one balloon for each member of your group. When kids arrive, hand out the balloons. Announce that group members will be competing in a balloon-popping contest. As kids pop their balloons by sitting on them, assign each person a number—the first person to pop his or her balloon is #1; the second person is #2; and so on. After all of the balloons are popped, have kids line up according to their numbers; then have them read the slips of paper that were in their balloons in the order in which they're lined up. It's likely that the resulting "story" won't make any sense. Afterward, say: **When we gossip—talk about people and events at random—the result is often similar to what just happened with our story. It gets all messed up and makes no sense. The story may sound funny at first, but it really isn't. That's one of the reasons the Bible tells us not to gossip.**

### Step 5

After your kids have come up with positive things to say about each other and have shared those statements, instruct them to do the same thing for God. Read Psalm 46:10 aloud; then allow a few minutes of silence for kids to think about God. Have them think of at least one thing that they really love about God—encourage them to be creative here; then allow time for them to share what they thought of with at least one other person in the room. After a few minutes, call the group back together and ask volunteers to share something they heard about God that they may not have thought of themselves. Close the session with a time of prayer, praising God for all of the wonderful things He is.

MOSTLY
**GIRLS**

MOSTLY
**GUYS**

EXTRA
**FUN**

## Step 2

With a group of mostly girls, you'll probably need to make some changes to the skit on Repro Resource 8. For your purposes, Gossip Gus becomes Gossip Gertrude. Gertrude's friends are Bertha, Opal, and Thelma instead of Bert, Orville, and Thurman. Prudence, the girl Gus likes, becomes Dudley, the guy Gertrude likes. The rest of the storyline may remain the same. If your girls enjoy performing, you might want to bring in some costume clothing to help them really get into the skit.

## Step 5

Hand out pencils and slips of paper, making sure that each of your girls gets one fewer slip than the number of girls in the group. Instruct your group members to write a nice note to each person in the room (excluding themselves), sharing at least one nice thing about that person. When they're finished, allow time for them to deliver their notes to each other. Afterward, explain that we all need practice in sharing nice things about each other, both when the other person's not around and when he or she *is* around. The more we learn to concentrate on the positive, the more natural it will be for us to say positive things.

## Step 1

Your guys may not be adept at storytelling, but they probably like to hear stories that are incredible and barely believable. Ask: **What's the most unusual or fantastic true story you've ever heard?** If your guys don't mention any, have ready some "urban legends" to tell. (Examples include the lady who bought a "special breed of Chihuahua" that turned out to be a giant rat and the "choking Doberman"—discovered by a woman returning home and rushed to the vet where part of a finger was found stuck in his throat, leading to the discovery of a burglar passed out in the woman's home.) There are many more of these stories, and perhaps your guys will know several of them. They are almost always told as true stories, but are yet to be proven. Your guys may be especially vulnerable to this form of gossip.

## Step 2

After the skit on Repro Resource 8, ask: **Gus was a guy, but don't you think *girls* are really the ones who tend to gossip the most?** As group members respond, ask for specific examples. If you're clever and subtle about this, soon you can have your guys gossiping about girls, which will demonstrate that guys *are* just as prone to gossip as girls are.

## Step 1

Begin the session by having group members create a skit titled "An Average Day in the Land of Gossip." Explain that your kids have surely seen some of these natives. They're called Gossipers. So in other words, the skit should be what life would be like if everyone was a blatant gossiper. Your group members can have any job they wish in the Land of Gossip, but whenever they meet, they must act like Gossipers. This skit should be somewhat scary as kids see what could happen if gossip is allowed to occur unchallenged. It's not usually a pretty sight.

## Step 4

As you're discussing what constitutes gossip, explain that sometimes the difference between "gossip" and "not gossip" consists of only a few adjectives and adverbs. For example, take the statement "John took Mary out to dinner, to a movie, and then back home." This statement may be pure fact. But in the hands of an experienced gossiper, it can quickly become, "Smooth John took desperate Mary to a romantic movie, and then on a steamy ride back home." What began as an innocent statement can soon become juicy gossip. Let volunteers make a number of other innocent statements. After each one, work as a group to add a word or two to create gossip out of the statement. Afterward, explain (jokingly) that since group members have been able to create gossip in a nondestructive setting, perhaps they won't feel the need to do so outside the group.

## Step 2

Play one of the following video scenes:.
• *Bye, Bye, Birdie.* Play the musical number "Goin' Steady," in which a series of teenagers gossip over the phone about what happened on a date.
• *The Music Man.* Show the scene in which the River City women, who have been gossiping about the town librarian, sing "Pick a Little, Talk a Little." The number, which compares the women with chickens that are pecking at feed, concludes as a barbershop quartet joins in with "Good Night, Ladies."

After showing the scene, ask: **How does the word "gossip" apply to what these people were doing? Does the movie make gossip look dangerous, fun, silly, or what? How do kids today gossip in real life?**

## Step 4

Bring copies of "gossip columns" from newspapers or entertainment magazines. Such columns usually feature "insider" looks at who was seen with whom at a social event, whose career is in trouble, etc. Let small groups look the columns over. Ask: **Which of the items in each column might qualify as gossip? Which items could be destructive? If your school newspaper had a "gossip column," what kinds of information might it contain? If you were in charge of that column, what kinds of information would you want to keep out of it? Why?**

## Step 1

Replace Steps 1 and 2 with a shorter opener. Before the session, get three group members to agree to spread rumors as kids are arriving at your meeting place. Each rumormonger will try to spread a different rumor. All of the rumors should be believable and should at least be approved by you if you don't supply them. (Examples might include the following: "[Name of group member] isn't here this week because she got grounded"; "They got Mrs. [name of a woman in your church] to do our refreshments this week, and all she made was spinach dip"; "The church board found out that [your name] lied on his job application, and they're having a meeting to decide whether to fire him [or her]." Delay your entrance for a couple of minutes. When you finally arrive, ask how many believed each of the rumors and why. Did any of the rumors change or become more detailed as they were passed along? Be sure to dispel the rumors before moving on to Step 3.

## Step 3

Skip Repro Resource 9. Brainstorm ways in which each of the following little words could cause trouble, depending on how and when they were used: *fire, OK,* and *ugly.* (Examples might include the following: Yelling "Fire!" in a crowded room when there isn't any; saying "OK" to a boyfriend or girlfriend who wants to have sex; answering "Ugly," when another student asks what your math teacher is like.) Use these examples as you discuss the power of the tongue. In Step 4, use just the first five situations on Repro Resource 10.

## Step 2

To give your kids an idea of how prominent gossip is in our society, bring in some tabloid newspapers that feature outrageous stories about celebrities. Read a few of the headlines to your group members. Then say: **By now, most of us know not to believe what we read in the tabloids. But what if we didn't know that? What if people thought that these stories were true? What might be some of the effects in these peoples' lives?** As a group, brainstorm some of the far-reaching results of gossip in the lives of the celebrities featured in the tabloids. Use this activity to lead in to Step 3.

## Step 4

Ask your group members to share some examples of how gossip negatively affected someone they know. Without using names, have kids explain what happened in the person's life as a result of being gossiped about. If possible, be prepared to share an example of your own. Be careful, however, not to let this activity turn into a gossip session!

**PLANNING CHECKLIST**

## Step 2
After the skit, divide your group into teams of five, making sure that you have a mix of junior highers and high schoolers on each team. Explain that each group member is to assume the role of one of the characters (other than the narrator) in the skit and answer the appropriate question below.
• Gus: What is it that makes you want to gossip?
• Bert: How did you feel when you kept hearing Gus change his story?
• Orville: How did you feel when you heard Gus talking about you?
• Thurman: Do you think Gus is a friend that you can trust? Why or why not?
• Prudence: Why did you say you wouldn't want to go out with Gus?
Let kids discuss their responses briefly in their teams. Then, if time permits, call the group back together and have all of the "Gus" characters share their responses, all of the "Bert" characters share their responses, and so on.

## Step 4
After working through Repro Resource 10 to make sure that your junior highers are clear on the definition of "gossip," call for some volunteer high schoolers who are willing to share some of their "gossip" experiences with the group. You may even wish to set up a panel of "experts" who would be willing to talk about how they've felt when they were the target of gossip, what's happened when they've been involved in the spreading of gossip, how gossip changes between junior high and high school, and so on.

## Step 4
To make Repro Resource 10 more interesting for your sixth graders, try the following option. Each time you read a situation from the sheet, choose one of your group members to be the first person mentioned in that situation; that person will then grab a second group member to be the second person in the situation, and so on, according to the number of people needed. These kids will then arrange themselves (linking arms, facing off, etc.) to illustrate the "chain of communication" in that situation, to help your group visualize it.

## Step 5
As you wrap up the session, give each of your group members a parting gift—a small, inexpensive squirt gun—as a reminder to put out the "sparks" caused by gossip.

**Date Used:**

Approx.
Time

**Step 1: Say What?** _____
o Extra Action
o Small Group
o Large Group
o Heard It All Before
o Fellowship & Worship
o Mostly Guys
o Extra Fun
o Short Meeting Time
Things needed:

**Step 2: Gossip Gus** _____
o Mostly Girls
o Mostly Guys
o Media
o Urban
o Combined Junior High/High School
Things needed:

**Step 3: Big Results** _____
o Extra Action
o Little Bible Background
o Short Meeting Time
Things needed:

**Step 4: What's Gossip?** _____
o Small Group
o Large Group
o Extra Fun
o Media
o Urban
o Combined Junior High/High School
o Sixth Grade
Things needed:

**Step 5: Anti-Gossip** _____
o Heard It All Before
o Little Bible Background
o Fellowship & Worship
o Mostly Girls
o Sixth Grade
Things needed:

## YOUR GOALS FOR THIS SESSION:

*Choose one or more*

☐ To help kids recognize the damage that can be caused by lying.

☐ To help kids understand why God can't stand lying.

☐ To help kids choose a lifestyle of truth.

☐ Other _____
   _____

## Your Bible Base:

Exodus 20:16
Acts 4:32—5:11
Hebrews 6:18

**STEP 1**

# Tabloid Teasers

*(Needed: Tabloid newspapers, prizes [optional])*

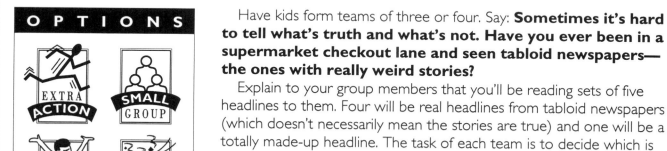

**O P T I O N S**

Have kids form teams of three or four. Say: **Sometimes it's hard to tell what's truth and what's not. Have you ever been in a supermarket checkout lane and seen tabloid newspapers—the ones with really weird stories?**

Explain to your group members that you'll be reading sets of five headlines to them. Four will be real headlines from tabloid newspapers (which doesn't necessarily mean the stories are true) and one will be a totally made-up headline. The task of each team is to decide which is the made-up headline. Emphasize to group members that they need to listen carefully, because you won't repeat any of the headlines.

After reading all five headlines in a set, give the teams about thirty seconds to decide; then have them verbalize their guesses. After all teams have registered their responses, announce the actual made-up headline. Have the teams keep track of how many they get right. Afterward, you might want to award prizes to the winning team.

Here are some headlines you might use (or you might want to come up with some of your own). The made-up headlines have an asterisk (*) next to them.

"2,000-Year-Old Mummy Wakes Up and Stabs Scientist"
"Do-It-Yourself Doc Operates on His Own Brain"
* "Man Bursts into Flames after Eating Mysterious Enchilada"
"Girl Hides 13 Years Over Bad Grades"
"Docs Attach Man's Foot to His Arm"

"Hubby Sues for Divorce Over Baby's Big Nose"
"U.S. Pilots Fly Captured UFO's in Nevada"
"Boy, 2, Swallowed by Giant Catfish"
"Woman Hasn't Slept a Wink in 30 Years"
* "Lovestruck Surgeon Leaves Love Letter inside Patient"

* "Housewife Cracks Egg for Breakfast and Finds Live Chirping Chick"
"Teen Sues Parents Because He's a Nerd"
"Ear Found in Jar of Spaghetti Sauce"
"Leech Saliva Is Miracle Drug for Heart Victims"
"Hungry Kitty on Death Row in Wisconsin for Stealing Food"

"Ouch! Fleeing Thief Shoves Lobster Down His Pants"
* "Flooded Raging River Carries Live Infant 30 Miles into Next State"
"World War II Bomber Found on the Moon"
"Cop Shoots Student During Gun-Control Lecture"
"Man Lives 52 Years with Axe Blade in His Head"

"Amazing Dog Girl Has 200 I.Q. and Talks with Animals"
"Five Ants Save Life of Abandoned Child"
"Hypnotized Dog's Testimony Nails Killer"
* "Woman's Wig Shrinks Until It Crushes Her Head"
"Thief Freezes in His Tracks—in Stolen Pair of Wet Jeans"

As a "bonus round," have teams guess which of the following is the *real* headline (indicated by an asterisk [*]).

"10 Die in Cookie Taste-Test Tragedy"
"Hijacking Terrorist Sobs, 'All I Wanted Was Another Bag of Peanuts' "
"Bank Teller Loses Arm in Drive-Thru Suction Tube"
* "Neighbors Chip in to Pay Loud Snorer $10,000 to Move Away"
"Restaurant Manager Fired for Making Mustard and Ketchup Shakes"

STEP
2

# Lots-o-Liars

*(Needed: Copies of Repro Resource 11, pencils)*

Ask: **Do you know junior highers who lie?** (Of course!)
Then say: **It seems like lying is pretty common among junior highers. It's during the junior high years that many people get "good" at lying. And then it becomes so much a part of who they are that they end up lying all through their lives.**

Hand out copies of "Lots-o-Liars" (Repro Resource 11) and pencils.
Say: **Many people agree that some lies are OK. But very few people agree on where to draw the line between an "OK lie" and a "bad lie." Read through the lies on this sheet and rank them from most OK (1) to worst (10).**

Allow group members to work in pairs to complete the sheet, if they wish. After about five minutes, have volunteers share their rankings. Which lies did they think were the worst? Which lies did they think were the "most OK"? Ask your volunteers to explain their rankings.

# Lie 'til Ya Die!

*(Needed: Bibles)*

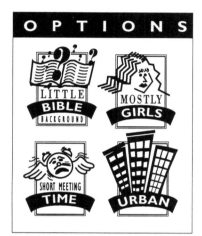

Say: **We like to think that some lies are OK and others a big deal. We even talk about "little white lies." But God makes it clear in the Bible that He's not fond of any lies!**

Have kids form small groups. Then have them turn in their Bible to Acts 4:32. As group members follow along, read Acts 4:32–5:11. This passage is the story of Ananias and Sapphira, a married couple who both lied to Peter (and to the Holy Spirit) and dropped dead on the spot as a result.

After you read the passage, give the groups about three minutes to put together a short skit depicting the story of Ananias and Sapphira. (Many junior highers will enjoy this because it's got a couple of pretty wild dying scenes.) As kids work, circulate among the groups to help them as needed. After a few minutes, have each group perform its skit.

Afterward, ask: **Why did Ananias and Sapphira die? Do you know of anyone who's ever died because he or she lied? How serious do you think God is about lying?** Get several responses.

# God's Character

*(Needed: Clear jar or container, water, vegetable oil)*

Have group members turn to Exodus 20:16. Ask one person to read aloud the verse. (This is the "Don't give false testimony" commandment.) Point out that telling the truth is such a big deal to God that He included it in the Ten Commandments.

Ask: **Why does God care if we lie or tell the truth?** (Because lying is a sin; because the Bible says not to lie.) If no one mentions it, point out that God is truth, so non-truth (or lying) is completely opposite of everything He is.

Ask: **Do you think it's possible for God to lie?** Of course your group members know that God *doesn't* lie, but they might struggle with whether or not He *can* lie.

Have group members turn to Hebrews 6:18. Ask one person to read aloud the verse, which says that it's impossible for God to lie.

Take out a clear jar or similar container. Fill it about half full with water. Then say: **Let's pretend that this water represents God.**

Then pull out a bottle of vegetable oil. Say: **This oil represents lying.** Pour a couple inches of oil on top of the water. Then put the lid on the jar and ask a volunteer to shake the ingredients together.

Afterward, say: **Just like this oil and water, God's truth and lying can never mix and will never mix—not even a little bit. So if we want to grow in our relationship with God, we need also to separate ourselves from lying and go for truth.**

# Truth Practice

*(Needed: Copies of Repro Resource 12, pencils)*

Say: **OK, so you're going to try to tell the truth. But sometimes people tell the truth and are real jerks about it. Let's get a little practice in telling the truth without being jerks.**

Hand out copies of "Truth Practice" (Repro Resource 12). Group members should still have pencils from the Repro Resource 11 activity (and, by now, have probably used them to turn that repro sheet into a nice vegetable strainer). Instruct your group members to respond honestly, and not to write down simply what they think is the "right" answer. Encourage them to think about how they would actually handle the situation. After about five minutes, ask a couple of volunteers to share their responses to each situation.

Close the session in prayer, asking God for strength for your group members to pursue truth.

# LOTS-O-LIARS

*Rank the following lies from the "most OK" (1) to the "worst" (10).*

_____ On his tax form, a man claims that he gave $2,000 to his church. He really gave $200.

_____ A man thinks his wife's dress looks really dorky, but he tells her she looks wonderful.

_____ A seventh-grade girl tells her parents that her homework is all done. It's really not, but she'll be able to finish it tomorrow morning in study hall.

_____ A seventeen-year-old boy tells his parents that no one came over while they were out of town. He really had a wild party with about fifty other kids from his school.

_____ A pastor exaggerates a story about something that happened to him to make his sermon sound good.

_____ An eighth-grade boy tells his dad that he has no idea how the garage door got all those dents in it. Actually, the boy and his friend had been shooting a BB gun at a target on the door the day before.

_____ A woman makes a long-distance personal phone call at work, then tells her boss it was work-related.

_____ A little boy with chocolate evidence all over his face and hands tells his mom that he wasn't in the cookie jar.

_____ A man calls in sick to work so that he can go fishing.

_____ A junior high girl tells her best friend that she has to do homework tonight so her friend won't be hurt that she's having a couple of other friends over to watch a video.

# TRUTH PRACTICE

### Situation 1

The rule in your house is "Absolutely no friends in the house when Mom and Dad aren't home." Your best friend drops by to give you some CDs while your parents are gone and ends up staying two hours. Later, your mom asks you where the CDs came from. How do you respond?

### Situation 2

Your friend has huge ears—and everybody is aware of it. She gets a new haircut that's supposed to hide them, but she's not happy with it. She says, "This haircut doesn't help at all. My ears still make me look like an ugly dork, don't they?" She's right. How do you respond?

### Situation 3

You and your friend get permission to go to a really cool concert on a school night. The next morning you remember a homework assignment that's worth one quarter of your total grade. The teacher clearly said that all late assignments will be marked down a whole grade. Your friend lies and tells the teacher that he was at an uncle's funeral. The teacher believes him and gives him two extra days to finish. Now the teacher asks for your assignment. How do you respond?

## EXTRA ACTION

### Step 1

Have kids stand along a wall. You'll ask each person a question to which you know the answer (the person's name, state capital, etc.). As soon as you ask, the person must decide whether to tell the truth or not. If the person tells the truth, he or she must run to the opposite left corner as you run in pursuit with a stuffed sock, trying to "bop" him or her. A prize (candy bar, gum, etc.) awaits the truth-teller in the corner. If the person lies, he or she is not chased, but walks to the opposite right corner, where no prize awaits. After giving everyone a turn, ask: **Was it worth it to tell the truth, even if you might get bopped? Why? In real life, how might telling the truth get you "bopped"? How might lying seem like an easy way to avoid getting bopped? What "prize" awaits those who tell the truth?**

### Step 4

Instead of using oil and water, have kids form two teams. Put each team on one end of a length of gift-wrap ribbon. Have kids play tug-of-war. As they do, say: **Sometimes we struggle over whether to tell the truth. We go back and forth about how much truth to tell. We think we can mix a little lying with a little truth and come out OK. But God doesn't struggle. His answer is clear.** Pull out scissors and cut the ribbon in the middle, sending the teams sprawling. (If your floor is hard, pre-pad the area with mats or cushions.) **God's answer is to tell the truth.**

## SMALL GROUP

### Step 1

Rather than using the tabloid-headline exercise as written, let kids play as individuals and compete against each other. Don't group the headlines as is done in the session. Rather, explain that some of them are actual headlines and others are made up. Hand out paper and pencils. Instruct kids to number their papers from 1 to 30. Read one headline at a time as kids decide whether to mark it "true" or "false." Afterward, go through the items a second time, revealing which ones are true and letting kids grade their papers. Award a prize to the winner, if you wish.

### Step 2

For a small group, try to make the exercise on Repro Resource 11 more personal. Rather than having kids simply rank the statements in order, ask the questions aloud by phrasing them as follows: "Have you ever . . . ?" or "Might you ever . . . ?" To respond affirmatively, kids should stand. To answer negatively, they should sit. After each question, let group members explain and/or defend their answers. Challenge everyone to be completely truthful. (After all, you're discussing lying.) Add other situations to the list that you know are issues your group members struggle with.

## LARGE GROUP

### Step 2

Have kids form groups. Ask the members of each group to brainstorm some possible results of finding out that the following people are chronic liars who hardly, if ever, tell the truth: your dentist, your doctor, the writers of your history book, a driver's ed instructor, your math teacher, the mayor of your city, your parents, your boyfriend or girlfriend, your Sunday school teacher or youth group leader, etc. (add others, as desired). Encourage kids to be creative and humorous as they consider possible results. (For example, if the writers of your history book are chronic liars, then you don't know for sure who was the first president of the United States.) After a few minutes, have each group share its results. Then go through Step 2 as written in the session.

### Step 5

Have kids form three or four groups. For each situation on Repro Resource 12, instruct each group to think of a possible reponse for the person involved and explain what the consequences of that response might be. One group should think of a truthful response and explain what the consequences of telling the truth might be. The other groups should think of lying responses and explain what the consequences of those lies might be. After a few minutes, have each group share its responses and consequences.

### Step 2

Kids who have gone through "values clarification" in school may find the situations on Repro Resource 11 rather tame. For example, what if you were hiding Jews from Nazis, and some Nazis asked whether you were hiding anyone? Is it OK to lie to save someone's life? You won't be able to settle that issue in this session, but you can acknowledge it. As needed, point out that the mother and sister of Moses hid his identity to protect him (Exodus 1–2); David faked insanity to save his own life, but did not exactly tell a lie (I Samuel 21). Others who lied outright to save their own skins (like Abraham in Genesis 12 and Peter in Matthew 26) are portrayed as having sinned. Even if a rare life-and-death situation justifies lying (and Christians may disagree over whether it does), it doesn't follow that giving "false testimony against your neighbor" (Exodus 20:16) is sometimes OK. Most of us are tempted to lie to save ourselves embarrassment, loss, or punishment—not to save lives.

### Step 4

If your kids are familiar enough with the Bible to know that God opposes lying, a reading of Exodus 20:16 may not make much of an impression on them. Instead, challenge kids to prove to *you*, using their Bibles and a couple of concordances you supply, that God is against lying. Have kids work in teams. The team to come up with the greatest number of supporting passages in five minutes wins. (A few examples might include Leviticus 6:1-5; Numbers 23:19; Psalm 5:6; Proverbs 6:19; 19:5, 9; 30:8; John 8:44; Romans 1:25; Colossians 3:9; Titus 1:2; and I John 2:21.)

### Step 3

Be sensitive to the implications of the Ananias and Sapphira story. If your kids don't know much about the Bible, it's preferable to teach the rewards of truthfulness rather than begin with a somewhat extreme liars-will-be-struck-dead passage. You might want to consider discussing Daniel's truthfulness even during desperate times (Daniel 6); the honesty of the thief on the cross (Luke 23:32-43); Solomon's heartfelt request for wisdom (I Kings 3:1-15); and similar examples.

### Step 5

If your group members are struggling a bit as they redefine their concept of lying, let them add situations from their own experience for group consideration. For example, they might ask, "Was it wrong for me to tell my parents I was at the library when I did indeed stop there for five minutes on the way to my best friend's house?" "Is it wrong for my friend to tell the teacher that his homework is his own even if he copies it from me himself?" Challenge kids to begin to deal with the *absolute* truth, but make sure to review Ephesians 4:15 and emphasize the importance of speaking that truth *in love*.

### Step 1

Begin the session by reading—and having your kids act out—the children's book *Max and the Big Fat Lie* (available from Chariot Books at your local Christian bookstore). Ask for volunteers to portray the following characters (listed in order of appearance): Max's friend Stevie, Max, Sir Fib, Max's mom, Kleever Deceiver, and Big Fat Lie. As you read the story, encourage kids to really play up their parts. Afterward, say: **Though this is a fun children's book, it contains a good truth about our topic today—lying. Often, once we start a lie, it snowballs out of control. How many of you can think of a time when that happened to you?** Get a few responses. **What are some reasons, other than the "snowball effect," that you can think of for not lying?** Allow time for responses. Then say: **Today we're going to take a look at what God thinks of lying.**

### Step 5

Read Proverbs 12:22 as further evidence that God *really* doesn't like it when we lie. Then have group members take a few minutes to brainstorm a list of all of the true things about God that they can think of. As they call out their truths, write them on the board. Encourage kids to consider the many different aspects of God and His personality. Close the session with a circle prayer. Have kids sit in a circle on the floor. One by one, have them thank God for each of the true things about Him that you listed on the board. If you run out of either kids or attributes, repeat prayers or prayers as needed.

## Step 3

If there are no guys in your group to play the male roles in Acts 4:32–5:11, recruit some volunteers from another group for this part of the session. If that doesn't work, bring in some props for your girls to use—old, oversized clothes; fishing gear or tools that might depict the occupations of some of the men; and so on. Be creative! Encourage your girls to really get into this story. It's an amazing account, one that is very clear about how God feels about lying.

## Step 5

Change the situations on Repro Resource 12 as follows:
• *Situation #1*—You and your best friend are going shopping. You're both trying to find a swimsuit. Ugh! You've looked in several stores. She tries on one that you think is the most hideous thing you've ever seen. She's convinced it's the one for her and tells you so. How do you respond?
• *Situation #3*—You and some of your friends are going out for pizza and then to a movie. You're planning to see the newest animated release from Disney, but when you get to the theater, your friends decide to go see a very steamy love story that your parents have specifically said you can't see. You go with your friends to see the love story. When you get home, your mom asks how the movie was. How do you respond?

## Step 2

Help your guys be more open about lying by making a contest out of it. For example, begin by having them compete to describe "The Biggest Lie I Ever Told—and Got Caught In." Then have a second round in which group members describe "The Biggest Lie I Ever Told and Got Away With." Award prizes if you wish, or perhaps create a "Forked Tongue" award for your winners. Then ask: **Why do many guys seem to take such pride in "getting away with" lying and similar behavior that isn't at all honorable?**

## Step 4

Ask: **Do you know a guy who never lies?** Most guys will probably think of at least one trustworthy person. **If so, what kind of person is he? Would you like to be that kind of person—someone whom everybody could trust? If so, how do you think you go about becoming that kind of guy?** Point out that integrity isn't established overnight. Explain that lying will eventually have results. Even if it seems like your guys are getting away with it now, lying will eventually catch up with them. If your guys ever want to be respected and have other people feel at ease to discuss problems and seek help from them, they will have to stop lying *now* and start building a trustworthy reputation.

## Step 1

Begin the session with a game of "To Tell the Truth." Call for three volunteers at a time. The three should quickly decide on something embarrassing, funny, or unique that one of them has done—and that other group members will not know about. Have them stand before the rest of the group as all three announce, "I shook hands with the president when I was six years old" (or whatever they've decided on). Let the other group members quiz each of the volunteers, trying to determine which of the three is telling the truth. For example, they might ask, "Which president was it?" "What was the temperature in Washington when you were there in April?" After a few questions, ask: **How many people think Person #1 is telling the truth? How many think Person #2 is telling the truth? How many think Person #3 is telling the truth?** Let your truth teller identify himself or herself.

## Step 5

As you wrap up the session, say: **I want to see how much you've been learning about detecting lying and the importance of telling the truth.** Before the session, write out a lengthy list of statements about yourself. Read one at a time; let kids write down whether they think each statement is true or false. (All of the statements should be true, but don't let on. To make this work, you will need to recall as many interesting and exciting things about yourself as you can. Many statements should sound so outlandish, or deal with sides of you that kids don't normally see, that they assume such statements must be false.) When you reveal that everything you said was true, point out that we need not lie to create fun and excitement in life. The truth can be plenty thrilling if we stick to it and commit to being truthful with each other.

MEDIA

SHORT MEETING TIME

URBAN

## MEDIA

### Step 1

Show some of the following video scenes (after pre-screening them for appropriateness):

• *In the Line of Fire.* Show the scene in which John Malkovich's character opens a bank account under a false name, lying to a female employee about where he's from and what he does.

• *Dirty Rotten Scoundrels.* Play a scene in which Lawrence (Michael Caine) pretends to be an exiled king or in which Freddy (Steve Martin) claims to have an ailing grandmother.

• *The Freshman.* Show the scene in which Victor (Bruno Kirby) offers a ride to Clark (Matthew Broderick). Later, show what follows—Victor steals Clark's belongings.

• *Murder on the Orient Express.* Play a scene in which any of the suspects (Ingrid Bergman, Lauren Bacall, Sean Connery, Vanessa Redgrave, John Gielgud, Anthony Perkins, etc.) denies involvement in the murder. As it turns out, they *all* did it.

After you show each scene, have kids vote on whether the character is telling the truth (all are lying). After you've shown all of the scenes, reveal the answers and award prizes to your best "lie detectors." Ask: **How can you tell whether someone is lying? What are the advantages of being a "good liar"? What are the disadvantages?**

### Step 5

Play a song in which one person bluntly confronts another with the truth. Examples might include "You're No Good" (Linda Ronstadt), "You're So Vain" (Carly Simon), "Young Girl" (Gary Puckett and the Union Gap), "Goodbye Yellow Brick Road" (Elton John), "Mr. Big Stuff" (Jean Knight), and "These Boots Are Made for Walkin'" (Nancy Sinatra). Then ask: **What truth was the singer trying to get across? Was the truth told in a loving way? What reaction would you have if the song were directed at you? How could you change the lyrics to tell the truth in a more loving way?**

## SHORT MEETING TIME

### Step 1

Try a shorter opener. As you start your meeting, announce that you can't say what the topic is. But you can give kids three hints. The first person to guess the topic will win a prize. At that point, stick a plastic fork in your mouth, tines out. Let it hang there while you tell kids that this is the first clue. Next, put down the fork and cover a group member's head with a towel for about ten seconds. Explain that this is the second clue. Finally, have a group member (with whom you've arranged this beforehand) suddenly jump up and yell "My pants are on fire!" before he or she runs out of the room. Explain that this is the third clue. See whether anyone can guess the topic. (First clue: Speaking with a forked tongue. Second clue: Cover-up. Third clue: "Liar, liar, pants on fire." The topic, of course, is lying.) In Step 2, instead of ranking the lies, simply have kids vote on whether each is "OK" or "not OK."

### Step 3

Rather than having kids come up with Ananias and Sapphira skits, simply have volunteers act out the story as you read the passage. In Step 5, use only Situation 2 from Repro Resource 12.

## URBAN

### Step 3

Ask volunteers to share some examples of how lying negatively affected someone they know. It may be that the person was lied about, was caught in a lie, or believed a lie of someone else. Without using names, have kids explain what happened in the person's life as a result of lying. If possible, be prepared to share an example of your own. After several group members have shared, introduce the story of Ananias and Sapphira, who suffered the ultimate negative consequence for lying.

### Step 5

Add the following situation to Repro Resource 12:

• Last night, the apartment next door to you was burglarized. Today, on the way home from school, you overhear a couple of gang members talking about the haul they got from the burglary. One of the guys pulls out a knife and threatens to "hurt you bad" if you tell anyone about what they said. When you get home from school, a police officer is canvassing the neighborhood, investigating the burglary. He asks you if you know anything about what happened last night. How do you respond?

### Step 1
Divide kids into two teams—junior highers versus high schoolers—for the headline contest. Instead of reading the headlines aloud to the teams, give each team several sets of the "real" headlines, making sure that each gets different headlines. Allow the teams several minutes to come up with their own fake headlines to add, one per set of "real" ones. To begin the game, have a representative from one team read its headlines to the other team. If the other team can guess which headline is made up, it receives a point. The team with the most points at the end of the game is the winner.

### Step 5
To get your kids used to responding truthfully in love and not just thinking about it, have them roleplay the situations presented on Repro Resource 12. The adult roles may be played by your high schoolers, but remember, they probably need as much practice in telling the truth as your junior highers. Go through each situation a couple of times, allowing different kids to respond differently. Then, as a group, discuss some of the options that were portrayed, as well as some that may have been overlooked.

### Step 2
Have kids form pairs. Give each pair several rubber bands. Read aloud the situations on Repro Resource 11. But instead of having kids rank the lies on a scale of one to ten, have partners stretch a rubber band to indicate how much they think each person on the sheet is "stretching the truth." If partners think a person is doing more than stretching the truth, they should pull their rubber band until it breaks.

### Step 5
Replace Situation 3 on Repro Resource 12 with the following:
• There's a phone call for you. It's Brandon, one of your best friends. "My mom doesn't believe that I was studying at the library with you last night," he says. "She thinks that I was at some party. Would you tell her the truth?" The truth is that Brandon *was* at a party last night and was *not* with you at the library. He hands the phone to his mom, who asks, "Was Brandon at the library with you last night?" How do you respond?

**Date Used:**

Approx. Time

**Step 1: Tabloid Teasers** _____
o Extra Action
o Small Group
o Fellowship & Worship
o Extra Fun
o Media
o Short Meeting Time
o Combined Junior High/High School
Things needed:

**Step 2: Lots-O-Liars** _____
o Small Group
o Large Group
o Heard It All Before
o Mostly Guys
o Sixth Grade
Things needed:

**Step 3: Lie 'til Ya Die!** _____
o Little Bible Background
o Mostly Girls
o Short Meeting Time
o Urban
Things needed:

**Step 4: God's Character** _____
o Extra Action
o Heard It All Before
o Mostly Guys
Things needed:

**Step 5: Truth Practice** _____
o Large Group
o Little Bible Background
o Fellowship & Worship
o Mostly Girls
o Extra Fun
o Media
o Urban
o Combined Junior High/High School
o Sixth Grade
Things needed:

# Custom Curriculum Critique

*Please take a moment to fill out this evaluation form, rip it out, fold it, tape it, and send it back to us. This will help us continue to customize products for you. Thanks!*

1.  Overall, please give this *Custom Curriculum* course (*Tongue Untwisters*) a grade in terms of how well it worked for you. (A=excellent; B=above average; C=average; D=below average; F=failure) Circle one.

    A     B     C     D     F

2.  Now assign a grade to each part of this curriculum that you used.

    | | | | | | | |
    |---|---|---|---|---|---|---|
    | a. Upfront article | A | B | C | D | F | Didn't use |
    | b. Publicity/Clip art | A | B | C | D | F | Didn't use |
    | c. Repro Resource Sheets | A | B | C | D | F | Didn't use |
    | d. Session 1 | A | B | C | D | F | Didn't use |
    | e. Session 2 | A | B | C | D | F | Didn't use |
    | f. Session 3 | A | B | C | D | F | Didn't use |
    | g. Session 4 | A | B | C | D | F | Didn't use |
    | h. Session 5 | A | B | C | D | F | Didn't use |

3.  How helpful were the options?
    - ❏ Very helpful
    - ❏ Somewhat helpful
    - ❏ Not too helpful
    - ❏ Not at all helpful

4.  Rate the amount of options:
    - ❏ Too many
    - ❏ About the right amount
    - ❏ Too few

5.  Tell us how often you used each type of option (4=Always; 3=Sometimes; 2=Seldom; 1=Never)

    | | 4 | 3 | 2 | 1 |
    |---|---|---|---|---|
    | Extra Action | ❏ | ❏ | ❏ | ❏ |
    | Combined Jr. High/High School | ❏ | ❏ | ❏ | ❏ |
    | Urban | ❏ | ❏ | ❏ | ❏ |
    | Small Group | ❏ | ❏ | ❏ | ❏ |
    | Large Group | ❏ | ❏ | ❏ | ❏ |
    | Extra Fun | ❏ | ❏ | ❏ | ❏ |
    | Heard It All Before | ❏ | ❏ | ❏ | ❏ |
    | Little Bible Background | ❏ | ❏ | ❏ | ❏ |
    | Short Meeting Time | ❏ | ❏ | ❏ | ❏ |
    | Fellowship and Worship | ❏ | ❏ | ❏ | ❏ |
    | Mostly Guys | ❏ | ❏ | ❏ | ❏ |
    | Mostly Girls | ❏ | ❏ | ❏ | ❏ |
    | Media | ❏ | ❏ | ❏ | ❏ |
    | Extra Challenge (High School only) | ❏ | ❏ | ❏ | ❏ |
    | Sixth Grade (Jr. High only) | ❏ | ❏ | ❏ | ❏ |

6.  What did you like best about this course?

7.  What suggestions do you have for improving *Custom Curriculum*?

8.  Other topics you'd like to see covered in this series:

9.  Are you?
    ❑ Full time paid youthworker
    ❑ Part time paid youthworker
    ❑ Volunteer youthworker

10. When did you use *Custom Curriculum*?
    ❑ Sunday School        ❑ Small Group
    ❑ Youth Group          ❑ Retreat
    ❑ Other _____

11. What grades did you use it with? _____

12. How many kids used the curriculum in an average week? _____

13. What's the approximate attendance of your entire Sunday school program (Nursery through Adult)? _____

14. If you would like information on other *Custom Curriculum* courses, or other youth products from David C. Cook, please fill out the following:

    Name: _____
    Church Name: _____
    Address: _____
    _____
    Phone: (____) _____

                    Thank you!